PUB STROLLS IN

SUFFOLK

Cyril Francis

COUNTRYSIDE BOOKS
NEWBURY BERKSHIRE

First published 2004
© Cyril Francis 2004
Revised and updated 2010

COUNTRYSIDE BOOKS
3 Catherine Road
Newbury, Berkshire

To view our complete range of books,
please visit us at
www.countrysidebooks.co.uk

ISBN 978 1 85306 845 4

Photographs by the author
Designed by Graham Whiteman

Produced through MRM Associates Ltd., Reading
Typeset by CJWT Solutions, St Helens
Printed by Information Press, Oxford

Contents

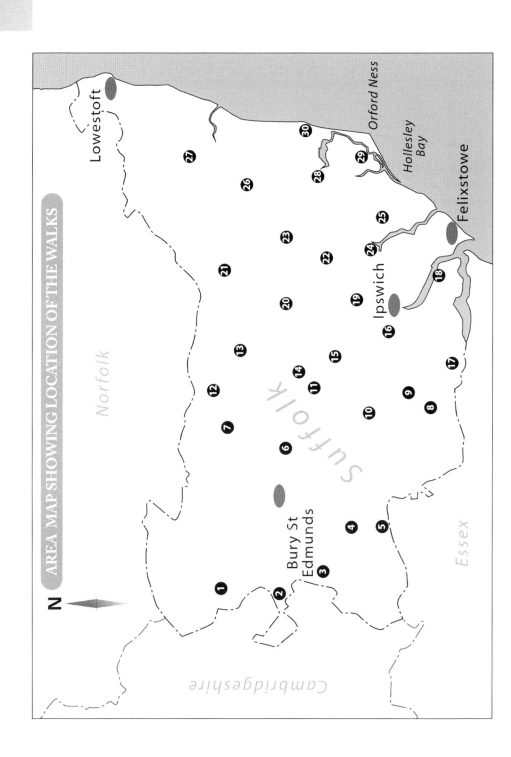

AREA MAP SHOWING LOCATION OF THE WALKS

PUBLISHER'S NOTE

We hope that you obtain considerable enjoyment from this book; great care has been taken in its preparation. Although at the time of publication all routes followed public rights of way or permitted paths, diversion orders can be made and permissions withdrawn.

We cannot, of course, be held responsible for such diversion orders and any inaccuracies in the text which result from these or any other changes to the routes nor any damage which might result from walkers trespassing on private property. We are anxious though that all details covering the walks are kept up to date and would therefore welcome information from readers which would be relevant to future editions.

The simple sketch maps that accompany the walks in this book are based on notes made by the author whilst checking out the routes on the ground. However, for the benefit of a proper map, we do recommend that you purchase the relevant Ordnance Survey sheet covering your walk. The Ordnance Survey maps are widely available, especially through booksellers and local newsagents.

Suffolk is a beautiful and historic place – there's no doubt about it. Hidden away in the towns and countryside are treasures that are best discovered on foot. Follow the strolls contained in this book and you will encounter diverse habitats such as heath and woodland, a shingle beach, a cliff top, river valleys, lush pasture and a deep ravine. Along the way, there is the opportunity to find isolated medieval churches, watch rare birds and butterflies, walk over an ancient packhorse bridge, explore a couple of famous castles, and learn about a gruesome murder.

The pubs have been selected on a geographical basis as well as for their access to scenic countryside. They come in all shapes and sizes; some with thatched roofs and others built of brick. Many have inglenook fireplaces, low ceilings and timber beams, often decorated with horse brasses. From the pictures hanging on the walls, you can sometimes discover a little of the pub's history and that of the local industry. I have included many establishments that do quality meals at reasonable prices and a few who offer the same but in more sophisticated surroundings. Most are used to walkers and, if booked beforehand, will willingly have a meal ready and waiting for you when you return from your stroll. It's appropriate perhaps to find that some of the featured pubs offer real ales brewed by two of Suffolk's best known brewers – Greene King (established in 1799) and Adnams (1872), based in Bury St Edmunds and Southwold respectively. Landlords do come and go, of course, so it's highly advisable to contact the pub in advance for details of opening times and when food is available. Generally speaking, car parking is not a problem. For security reasons and common courtesy, always be sure to let the publican know that you are leaving the car on his or her premises while you walk – and it goes without saying that you should also be a customer. You'll find most pub car parks quite roomy but, where appropriate, alternative parking arrangements are listed.

Most of the strolls follow a mixture of field edge paths, quiet lanes, bridleways and farm tracks, often through rolling countryside – with one or two climbs but nothing too serious – and the majority can be walked all year round, whether it be on a warm sunny day or when there is a sprinkling of frost on the ground. During inclement weather conditions, some paths become very sticky with mud so stout footwear is strongly recommended. It's best to take your boots off when you go into the pub, or carry a couple of plastic bags with you to place over them. Also, keep an eye on the weather and dress accordingly as some isolated stretches of countryside offer little or no protection against the elements.

Sketch maps accompany each route description. However, these carry only the minimum detail and it may be as well to take an Ordnance Survey map with you; the numbers of the relevant Explorer sheets (1:25 000) have been included.

Finally, enjoy strolling through the countryside in this lovely county and respect its life and work.

Cyril Francis

Worlington
The Walnut Tree

MAP: OS EXPLORER 226 (GR 696736)   WALK 1   DISTANCE: 3½ MILES

DIRECTIONS TO START: WORLINGTON VILLAGE LIES ABOUT ONE MILE SOUTH-WEST OF MILDENHALL ON THE B1102. **PARKING:** THERE IS A CAR PARK BESIDE THE PUB.

The start of the stroll is on the border of what is known as the Fens, a landscape noted for its flatness and rich peaty soils. This pleasant little circuit offers the opportunity to walk beside the slow-moving River Lark as it meanders its way through lush pasture to the market town of Mildenhall. An added attraction is Kings Staunch Cottage, a much-extended former lock keeper's cottage, where you cross the river by a narrow wooden bridge. In 1720 the Lark Navigation was constructed, which, amongst other things, allowed barges to deliver shipments of coal to Bury St Edmunds. Nowadays, water from the river is used mainly for land irrigation and recreation purposes. Aircraft from the nearby twin United States Air Force bases of Lakenheath and Mildenhall frequently shatter the relative peace and quiet. You can observe aircraft movements from special viewing areas situated by the roadside near each airfield.

The Walnut Tree

As pub origin dates go, the Walnut Tree must rate as one of the youngest in the book. The precise date of building is unknown, but from pictures of horse-drawn carriages passing by – long before the advent of popular motoring – it's thought that the pub dates from some time in the late 1800s. At first sight it looks like a large Victorian brick house. Standing beside the B1102, it's a handy place to call in for food and drink. Once inside, you'll find a light and airy bar lounge, with the furniture neatly arranged. The changing menu contains a selection of typical pub food – everything from light snacks to substantial meals. Smoked haddock, fresh cod, scampi, liver and bacon casserole, lasagne and steak and ale pie are just some of the popular dishes here, all freshly cooked. An à la carte menu is also available. Featuring among the lighter fare are sandwiches, ploughman's and baguettes. There is also a children's menu and a traditional roast is available on Sunday. You can eat in the bar or in the non-smoking restaurant, or outside in the large and very popular beer garden. The Walnut Tree is open during normal licensing hours except for Mondays, when it is closed all day. Telephone: 01638 713345.

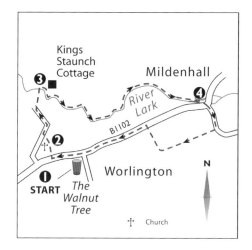

The Walk

① Turn left at the T-junction beside the pub and continue along the footway. Maintain direction for about 300 yards to pass the village hall and Holly House. Just past the latter, turn right onto a footpath beside some metal railings. Carry on along the path, which runs between hedgerows and shortly beside a graveyard.

② Pass through a small gate, go forward a few paces and turn right. Follow the path through All Saints' churchyard and exit the latter by a kissing gate. Turn right onto a minor road and walk to the far end. Turn left onto a cart track and follow it into a cultivated field. Go down the left side of the field and, after about 150 yards, turn right to take a cross-field path, which leads to Kings Staunch Cottage.

③ Cross the river by a wooden bridge to enter the cottage garden. Turn right here and leave by a kissing gate positioned just ahead. Turn right to walk beside the River Lark for the next mile or so, crossing the entrance to Wamil Hall in the process. Turn right when you reach a cinder path and soon pass an isolated cottage. Continue on a narrow bridleway and later fork right down a slope to regain the riverside. Pass the edge of a playing field and cross the river bridge. Just before the next bridge, go left up a slope to reach the road.

The Suffolk countryside

④ Turn right and continue to the next bend before crossing over to join Station Road. Pass the entrance of the old railway station, then turn right, about 100 yards short of a sharp left bend. Join a grass track, which leads straight ahead between reed and tree lined dykes. A much narrower path soon emerges, which shortly steers you round to the right in front of a fence. Cross the former rail track bed and carry on straight ahead to finally reach the B1102. Turn left and walk along the footway back to the Walnut Tree.

PLACES OF INTEREST NEARBY
The **Mildenhall & District Museum** contains a complete replica (the originals are kept in the British Museum) of the Mildenhall Treasure – a collection of 34 pieces of 4th-century Roman silverware. There are also galleries devoted to the history of RAF Mildenhall and a natural history display of Breckland. Telephone: 01638 716970.

Moulton
The Kings Head

DIRECTIONS TO START: LEAVE THE A14 JUST EAST OF KENTFORD AND TAKE THE B1506. AT KENTFORD TURN ONTO THE B1085, GOING SOUTHWARDS, AND FOLLOW THE SIGNS TO MOULTON. **PARKING:** AT THE SIDE AND REAR OF THE PUB.

The small community of Moulton is sheltered in the Kennett valley near the Cambridgeshire border, with the long distance Icknield Way path passing to the north of the village. Another interesting feature is the 15th-century packhorse bridge maintained by English Heritage. Steps were added in later years, to deter high-spirited Cambridge graduates from riding their motorcycles over the bridge. Nearby, posts with water depth markings on them suggest that the River Kennett is occasionally prone to flooding. Stone cottages fronting Brookside Lane and an arched bridge over the river form part of a peaceful and picturesque scene. The stroll itself is easily undertaken. Although setting off up a longish hill out of Moulton, you are rewarded with some spectacular views as you gently descend and return to the Kings Head.

The Kings Head

Not a great deal is known about the history of the original Kings Head, which is believed to have burnt down in the late 1800s. Standing not far from the packhorse bridge, it may have been used by travellers as they journeyed along the old route from Cambridge to Bury St Edmunds. After the fire, a new pub was built of brick – look carefully at the walls and you will see the decorative pattern of brickwork. In the summer months the exterior is given a splash of colour by flowers in hanging baskets and window boxes. Steps lead up to the front door and inside to the bar area, and in the adjoining room there is a small comfortable restaurant. This pub has changed hands of late. The incoming publican said that pub opening hours had yet to be finalised. He hoped to offer food – probably of the traditional pub grub variety – at a later date. Definitely one pub to telephone before visiting. Outside there is a delightful beer garden complete with a summertime awning. The pub is open seven days a week and food is available daily. Telephone: 01638 551844.

The Walk

① Head towards the packhorse bridge and learn something of its history from an interpretation board. Carry on straight ahead and proceed up the Gazeley road. Ahead of you is a steady climb of about 800 yards along a metalled surface. Go past the entrance to Primrose Hill Farm on the left.

② Just before the road bears left and power lines cross it, look right for a gap in

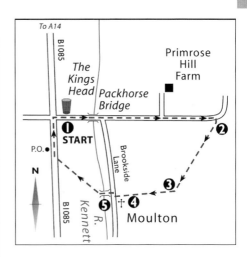

the hedge. Go up some steps in the bank and over a stile. Veer slightly right to join a cross-field path. Stay on the path, which later gives a panoramic view of the surrounding countryside, and shortly cross another stile. To the right on a clear day, the Cambridgeshire fens and the tower of Ely Cathedral can often be seen in the distance.

③ Keep on the descending path, with some of the village houses coming into view in the valley below. Carry on towards the field boundary and aim for a stile in the hedge. Cross the stile and continue on a

PLACES OF INTEREST NEARBY

Lackford Lakes Reserve, on the A1101 north-east of Kentford, is run by the Suffolk Wildlife Trust and contains a number of restored gravel pits, which have become wildlife havens for a variety of birds in both summer and winter. Butterflies, dragonflies and wild plants can also be found here. There is a visitor centre, along with waymarked trails and bird hides. Telephone: 01284 728706.

The packhorse bridge, Moulton

narrow downhill path, where overhanging trees provide a lovely tunnel effect.

④ With St Peter's church just ahead, cross over a boundary wall to join a gravel path in the graveyard. Pass the church on the left and exit by a metal kissing gate. (If you wish to extend the walk by a further 2 miles, turn left and walk to Catford Bridge beside the river – visible in places – and then retrace your steps.)

⑤ Turn right and follow Brookside Lane. Shortly, go left over an arched bridge and cross a stile to enter some pasture. With a paddock fence initially on the left, follow the path to reach the far boundary. Turn right when you reach the road and later pass the post office and general stores. At the road junction in front, turn right into Bridge Street. The Kings Head is just ahead on the left.

Lidgate
The Star Inn

MAP: OS EXPLORER 210 (GR 722578) **WALK 3** **DISTANCE:** 4½ MILES

DIRECTIONS TO START: LEAVE THE A14 AT KENTFORD. JOIN THE B1085 GOING SOUTH AND THEN THE B1063, WHICH FINALLY TAKES YOU TO LIDGATE. THE STAR IS ON THE LEFT SHORTLY AFTER ENTERING THE VILLAGE. **PARKING:** AT THE REAR AND SIDE OF THE PUB.

The village of Lidgate nestles in the Kennett valley amongst the chalky-clay soils of the Suffolk-Cambridgeshire border. Thatched cottages stand either side of a picture postcard street, including the attractive timber-framed Suffolk House, which dates from the 16th century and has gradually been restored. Ducks, geese and the occasional lone heron can often be found on the village pond. Features of this walk include a couple of lovely green lanes, with splendid views across the valley slopes and a delightful stretch beside the River Kennett. Towards the end of the walk, the path runs beside woodland, which provides additional greenery to a colourful agricultural landscape.

The Star Inn

At first glance, the Star looks like a wealthy merchant's house, which it may well have been before it became a pub, possibly in the 1830s. Step inside and you will soon discover that this is no ordinary Suffolk hostelry, but a source of wonderful western Mediterranean food. This is not the place to come for sandwiches and baguettes. Instead, chalked up on a blackboard hanging over a huge fireplace, you will find dishes such as prawns in garlic, Catalan salad, paella, moules marinière and parrillada – seafood stew. Other delicious main courses like chicken, lamb and venison are also cooked with a Spanish twist. The desserts include pavlova, bread and butter pudding and treacle pudding. Greene King IPA and Abbot are on offer, alongside Morland Old Speckled Hen and a choice of lagers. Wines mainly come from a Spanish wine list. Situated in the bar area are a billiards table and dartboard. The Star is open every day except Monday. Food is available daily except Sunday evenings. Well-behaved children are welcome. Booking is advisable for meals. Telephone: 01638 500275.

The Walk

① Turn left out of the pub and proceed along the footway. Just beyond, where the latter peters out, turn left into Bury Lane. Maintain direction until you reach the end of the surfaced road. Continue ahead on a grassy path, with a hedge on the right. Shortly, the path runs between a hedge and ditch on either side. Keep climbing gently uphill and turn left at a crossways, just before arriving at a tall mast.

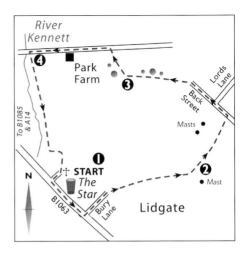

② Walk the length of the leafy green lane, with two masts ahead, and turn left when you reach the road. Continue to the next junction and carry straight on along a lesser road signposted to Back Street. Carry on for another 200 yards, past Meadow Cottage and shortly ignore a footpath going left. Keep forward, disregarding a farm access track going right, and afterwards join a descending earth lane. Carry on ahead and shortly lose the left-hand hedgerow. Stay beside the curving right side next to Beech Plantation and look for a broad entrance (unmarked) about halfway along.

③ Turn right here and follow a field edge path beside the Plantation to the bottom of

PLACES OF INTEREST NEARBY
The **National Horse Racing Museum** at Newmarket tells the story of horse racing through the museum's permanent collections, which feature memorabilia of leading jockeys and horses. You can dress up in silks before weighing out, and ride a horse simulator. Telephone: 01638 667333.

The tall mast

a slope. Go over a bridge in the corner, cross some pasture and, climb over a stile in the hedge opposite. Turn left here to join the Newmarket-Ousden road and continue steadily downhill. At the bottom turn left by a bridge over the River Kennett.

④ Go down some steps, then up a small bank and veer slightly right beside a rail fence. Stay near to the riverbank through successive fields to eventually cross a wooden bridge. Continue ahead and turn left opposite a road bridge on the right, to follow a gently rising grassy path. At the far boundary, turn left onto an earth track. Go right in front of the churchyard entrance to finally emerge beside the village pond. Turn left at the village pond and return to the Star, some 300 yards ahead.

Hawkedon
The Queens Head

MAP: OS EXPLORER 210 (GR 799531)　　**WALK 4**　　**DISTANCE:** 5 MILES

DIRECTIONS TO START: LEAVE THE A143 HAVERHILL-BURY ST EDMUNDS ROAD
JUST EAST OF CHEDBURGH AND FOLLOW SIGNS TO REDE, THEN CONTINUE
TO HAWKEDON, ABOUT 4 MILES FURTHER ALONG A MINOR ROAD.
PARKING: PARK BESIDE THE PUB.

The small village of Hawkedon is on the road to nowhere in particular. Blink, and you might miss it as you pass through. However, the scenic landscape alone is worth the effort to stop and explore. Also, the 15th-century parish church of St Mary is the only one in Suffolk with a walled churchyard that is surrounded by a village green on all four sides. This walk's undulating route passes through several stretches of hilly countryside, dispelling the often-held notion that Suffolk is flat. The highest point in the county – a mere 420 ft above sea level – can be found in the neighbouring village of Rede. Hidden surprises on the walk include some large fishing lakes, an isolated farmhouse at Purton Green and a ford.

The Queens Head

During the past few years, many rural communities have lost important services such as the post office, petrol station and, of course, the village pub. However, bucking the trend is the Queens Head, which has reopened after a spell of closure. The omens so far are good, and the stock of Wherry and Adnams favourites, plus four guest ales, has ensured that the pub is already popular with real ale enthusiasts. Included on the menu is a wide selection of dishes associated with a country pub. At present food is served on Wednesday and Thursday evenings. Lunches and suppers are available on Friday, Saturday and Sunday. The Queens Head has the feeling of a quintessential Suffolk hostelry, with its period furniture, massive brick fireplace, part wooden and tiled floor, and absence of fruit machines and jukebox. Photographs on the walls reflect village activities of yesteryear. From the beer garden outside, there are stunning views of the local countryside. The pub is open seven days a week. Telephone: 01284 789218.

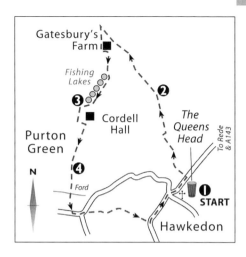

The Walk

① Turn right out of the car park and, in about 50 yards, turn left at Cresslands Corner. Go past the last bungalow on the left to join a winding farm access track. Ignore a path going right and enter some pasture. Pass a fishing lake on the right and enter a second stretch of pasture. Exit the latter by a metal gate and continue along the field edge with a ditch on the left.

② Pass a field entrance ahead and in

another 40 yards, turn left into a cultivated field. Bear right and follow the headland round to the top boundary. Go through a small spinney, veer right and continue on a diagonal cross-field path, aiming for a fingerpost on the other side. Turn left here onto a concrete driveway. Where the latter curves left to Gatesbury's Farm, carry on straight ahead on a broad grassy path. Keep following the path to where the hedge eventually finishes on the left. Turn right here to take the field path that descends to the bottom of a shallow valley. Go left after crossing a stile and pass a series of fishing lakes on the right.

③ Pass the last lake, turn right and head into a copse. Swing left and right to emerge into rough grassland. Follow the path to the corner, cross a ditch and turn left to join a farm track. Soon pass a partially-hidden, dilapidated cottage and ignore the concreted path leading to Cordell Hall. Continue on the track, shortly curving right and later accompanied by woodland on the right. Just after passing a small pond, turn left and pass through a belt of trees.

Purton Green farmhouse

④ With Pirton Green farmhouse appearing in front, turn right and take a descending field edge path, with a hedge on the left. Cross a ford at the bottom (over the bridge if necessary) and climb up the narrow access drive opposite. Turn left at the top and fork left at a road junction in front. Almost immediately, turn right to pass the ruined Stansfield Mill. Maintain direction, with a hedge on the left to reach the far corner. Turn left over a ditch and then go right over some rough ground to shortly walk beside Brook's Wood ahead.

PLACES OF INTEREST NEARBY
Clare Castle Country Park at Clare, 8 miles south of Hawkedon, is a 30-acre site containing the earthworks of a former Norman castle, along with a children's play area. The original goods van, which still stands on a section of dismantled railway line, acts a visitor information centre. Running beside the park is the River Stour. Telephone: 01787 277491.

Cross a stretch of cultivated field before turning left onto the road and returning to the pub.

Cavendish
The George

MAP: OS EXPLORER 196 (GR 803466)   **WALK 5**   DISTANCE: 3 MILES

DIRECTIONS TO START: CAVENDISH IS 8 MILES NORTH-WEST OF SUDBURY AND 3 MILES FROM LONG MELFORD ON THE A1092 ROAD BETWEEN CLARE AND LONG MELFORD. **PARKING:** THERE ARE A FEW PARKING SPACES IN FRONT OF THE GEORGE, OR IN THE SMALL PUB YARD.

With the splendid backdrop of St Mary's church and a group of pink-washed cottages huddled in front, the attractive village green at Cavendish is one the most painted and photographed scenes in the county. In 1381, during the Peasants' Revolt, Sir John Cavendish hung on to the handle of the church door to plead for sanctuary from his pursuers. Amazingly, the same door handle still hangs there over 600 years later. But the touristy village does have a darker side. Other notable features to be found on this inviting walk include the imposing building of Ducks Hall, standing at the bottom of a narrow winding lane. Later on, the high ground offers some fine views of the local landscape and of Cavendish itself.

The George

This welcoming 600-year-old pub stands beside Cavendish's splendid village green. Over the years the timber-framed building gradually deteriorated and was eventually boarded up. The present owners were apparently passing by one day and, realising its potential, purchased it and later carried out a programme of full refurbishment. The result is a delightful restaurant and bar area, where a unique character and individuality is much in evidence. An imaginative menu contains a wide choice including pasta, eggs, meat, poultry, fish and shellfish as well as delicious desserts. Light lunches are served from Monday to Saturday, and traditional roasts on Sundays. To complement the food there are real ales and an extensive wine list. The restaurant is non-smoking. Heated canopies in the walled garden allow dining al fresco all the year round. Children are welcome and booking is advisable for meals, especially at weekends. Telephone: 01787 280248.

The Walk

① Leave the George and turn left to walk through the village street, passing the post office. Go past the entrance to Water Lane, and soon turn left by a circular walk sign and a boundary wall to emerge onto a sports field. Continue straight ahead and turn right when you reach a four-finger signpost.

② Carry on along a grassy path that acts as a field break. Enter the adjoining field, turn right and shortly turn left to join a similar, well-defined path. Follow the rising

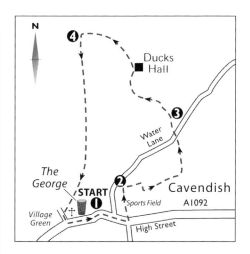

path to the far end, where it curves left and eventually leads to a minor road. Cross the road and take the narrow lane leading to Ducks Hall and The Leys as directed by a signpost.

③ Stay on the undulating lane to pass a thatched cottage on the right and afterwards the impressive building of Ducks Hall. Just past The Leys veer slightly left onto a small section of farm track. Take the next turning left and then quickly swing right to continue on a headland path, with a hedge on the right. Keep walking until you reach a wooden electricity pole, where you turn left onto a field break path, with some power cables running parallel.

PLACES OF INTEREST NEARBY

Melford Hall, Long Melford. A well-preserved Tudor House that has a long association with British naval heroes. Queen Elizabeth I and children's author Beatrix Potter are just two of the many well-known people who have visited the Hall. Telephone: 01787 379228.

Cavendish village green

④ The path initially rises, with good views of the countryside as you go over the brow of the field. Stay on the path as it heads in a straight line back towards the village. After passing the rear gardens of some nearby houses, the path narrows and shortly runs beside a long brick boundary wall. Cross a footbridge to enter St Mary's churchyard and bear left. Exit the churchyard by a wrought iron gate and make your way beside the village green back to the George.

Beyton
The White Horse

MAP: OS EXPLORER 211 (GR 935634)   **WALK 6**   **DISTANCE:** 3 MILES

DISTANCE TO START: BEYTON LIES JUST OFF THE A14 MIDWAY BETWEEN BURY ST EDMUNDS AND STOWMARKET. LEAVE THE A14 AT ONE OF THE SIGNPOSTED BEYTON TURN OFFS AND HEAD FOR THE VILLAGE. THE WHITE HORSE STANDS IN FRONT OF THE GREEN.
PARKING: IN THE LARGE CAR PARK BESIDE THE PUB OR IN FRONT OF THE GREEN.

The centre of the village at Beyton lies around the lovely triangular-shaped green, its attractions all the greater with the removal of the traffic some years ago to the nearby A14. After leaving Bury Road, this compact walk takes you into open countryside, along field edge paths beside thick hedgerows. Although you may be only a few minutes' walk away from the village centre, you could be miles from anywhere, such is the sense of quietness and solitude. Mature trees in Chevin's Wood and horses grazing in a paddock provide a scenic contrast. Near the village green you will probably encounter a gaggle of geese freely roaming the area. The geese are featured on the village sign and their presence shows no sign of abating.

The White Horse

This popular pub overlooks the village green and welcomes walkers. It used to cater for trade on the old A45, which passed by its door. As you walk through the passage by the back door, you pass a grill over a well – at one time, this may have contained fresh water, when perhaps the pub brewed its own beer. A date on one of the chimneys suggests that part of the building originated during the early 17th century. Delicious home-cooked food, which is served daily and normally eaten in the lounge bar, includes a good selection of starters, also roasts, steak and kidney pudding, toad in the hole, steaks and curries, with a variety of desserts to follow. For something lighter, ploughman's lunches are offered as well as a range of sandwiches filled with meats and salads. Traditional cask ales from the Greene King brewery are among the beers available. Outside there is a large beer garden with plenty of amusements for younger children. Opening times are during normal licensing hours and booking is advisable for meals. Telephone: 01359 270324.

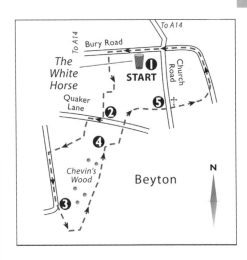

The Walk

① Leave the car park and turn left into Bury Road. Carry on until you reach the Beyton boundary signpost on the right. Turn left and go up some steps in the bank to join a field edge path. Further on, swing right and left beside the hedge. When some houses appear on the left, carry straight on along a broad path to reach Quaker Lane in front.

② Turn right and continue along the lane for another 250 yards. Turn left through a field entrance to follow a path, with a hedge on the left. At the corner of a wood, veer right on a path, which takes you to the field edge, and then rejoin Quaker Lane again. Turn left and continue along the lane to reach High House, where the lane turns right.

③ Bear left here to join a broad path, which shortly passes a large, partially dead oak tree. Over to the left is Chevin's Wood. When you are level with its boundary, turn left and shortly walk beside it. Keep following it round to enter the adjoining

PLACES OF INTEREST NEARBY

With its vast oval-shaped rotunda and curved wings, **Ickworth House** at Horringer, 3 miles south-west of Bury off the A143, is a most unusual building. It was created by Frederick, the eccentric 4th Earl of Bristol, to display art and furniture collected on his European tours. Sadly, he died before the realisation of his dreams. The house now belongs to the National Trust. Telephone: 01284 735270.

The village green at Beyton

field. Look right to see the tower of neighbouring Hessett church soaring above the fields. Stay on a path, still skirting the wood, to arrive at a horse paddock.

④ Turn right to walk between wire fences and finally pass left through a metal gate. Follow a short access track to Quaker Lane. Cross the latter and continue on a narrow path, which initially runs between a conifer hedge and a panel fence. Stay on the path to emerge in front of All Saints' church.

Although this is kept locked, access may be obtained from one of the keyholders listed in the porch.

⑤ For a short cut back to the pub, turn left into Church Road. Otherwise, enter the churchyard and pass the church. Go beside a panel fence and veer left by a marker post to eventually arrive at a field entrance. Continue ahead with a hedge on the left to reach the road. Turn left here to return to your start point.

Stanton
The Cock Inn

MAP: OS EXPLORER 230 (GR 968734) **WALK 7** **DISTANCE:** 3½ MILES

DIRECTIONS TO START: TAKE THE A143 BURY ST EDMUNDS-DISS ROAD AND LOOK FOR THE TURN OFF FOR STANTON, TO THE NORTH OF IXWORTH. FOLLOW THE SIGNS INTO THE VILLAGE. **PARKING:** PARK TO THE REAR OF THE PUB.

Take a look at the map and you will see that Stanton lies in the heart of the countryside surrounded by large cultivated fields. A windmill standing in Upthorpe Road, dating from 1751, was moved to its current site in the early 19th century – you can visit this on certain days and purchase some freshly ground flour. The stroll later edges away from Stanton and continues towards Shepherds Grove, an area where the US military occupied an airfield during the Cold War years. However, the most interesting feature on the stroll is an extraordinary deep ravine known locally as 'The Grundle'. Making your way along a series of steps cut into the slopes of the naturally formed gully, gives the effect of being on a switchback machine. In periods of severe drought, you can walk along the bottom from one end to the other.

The Cock Inn

From its size and prominent position in the main street, it's thought that the 16th-century Cock may have been a coaching inn, although details of the route covered are unknown. Over the years, the inn has undergone structural alterations and refurbishment. The large lounge bar has an area set aside for darts, which is a popular activity here. In a smaller room there is a pool table. You may eat in the bar or in the no-smoking restaurant, the latter containing original wooden beams, with plaster covering the wattle and daub walls. A selection of bar snacks includes jacket potatoes, sandwiches and baguettes. From the main menu you can choose from dishes such as steak, chicken, lasagne, cottage pie, steak and kidney pudding and battered cod, and daily specials are chalked up on a board. A variety of tempting desserts is also on offer. The bar is well stocked with real ales and beer. Food is available every day except on Mondays when the Cock is closed. Walkers and cyclists can expect a warm welcome and receive excellent hospitality. Telephone: 01359 250230.

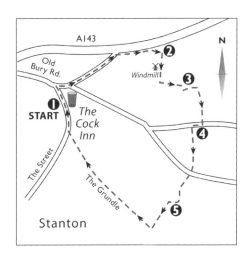

The Walk

① Leave the pub by the rear yard and pass through some concrete bollards to join Meadow Court. At the boundary bear left, walking across the road to join the old Bury road. Keep ahead on a footway for about 400 yards. When the road swings left at the approach of the A143, keep forward along a tarmac footpath that runs parallel to the main road.

② Follow the path and pass a property set back on the right. At a T-junction ahead, turn right onto Armstrong Avenue. Continue along the left grassy verge and turn left opposite house number 612A. Where the road bears right, carry on straight ahead along a track through a belt of woodland.

③ The track shortly swings right and left and later turns 90 degrees in front of a lone house. At the next brick building, come off the track and go down the right side of some grassland. Curve left at the bottom, go forward a few paces and turn right into the next field. With a hedge on the left, carry on to meet a road in front.

PLACES OF INTEREST NEARBY

For almost two centuries **Henry Watson's Potteries**, at Wattisfield, to the east along the A143, have been producing earthenware in the heart of the English countryside. Clay dug out of local earth helps to produce terracotta known as the 'Original Suffolk Collection'. Factory seconds are available to purchase on site. There's also a coffee shop and children's play area. Telephone: 01359 251239.

④ Veer slightly left and cross the road. Turn right at a field entrance and follow the field edge path beside the roadside hedge then bear left up the longer western boundary of the gradually narrowing field. Cross another road and a stile almost opposite. Carry on straight ahead, as directed by a footpath sign, over a culti- vated field. Cross into Wash Lane and turn right to join a broad bridleway.

⑤ Follow the bridleway to a corner and take a path as waymarked into a wooded area. This is the start of The Grundle. Stay on the path as it rises and falls along the sloping edges. After about 350 yards, just beyond a stretch of rail fence, exit the path and turn right onto a narrow lane. Follow the lane to a junction and turn right. In 100 yards, maintain direction to join The Street and return to the Cock.

The windmill at Stanton dates from 1751

Polstead
The Cock Inn

MAP: OS EXPLORER 196 (GR 994384) | **WALK 8** | **DISTANCE:** 3½ MILES

DIRECTIONS TO START: POLSTEAD LIES 5 MILES SOUTH-WEST OF HADLEIGH. LOOK FOR THE POLSTEAD TURN OFF ON THE A1071 AND FOLLOW THE SIGNPOSTS. THE COCK STANDS BESIDE THE VILLAGE GREEN. **PARKING:** PARK TOWARDS THE REAR OF THE PUB.

Situated on the northern slopes of the River Box valley, the small village of Polstead is a popular starting point for walkers – many consider the rolling countryside as some of the most attractive in the county. This compact circuit offers plenty of scope and variety, and in springtime the woodland floor is carpeted with wild flowers. An unusual feature is a sunken earth lane. The large village pond near the church, which attracts wildfowl, is a popular spot for anglers. Polstead is particularly remembered for two things: its cherry orchards, although harvesting is not what it used to be, and the gruesome murder of a local servant girl, Maria Marten, in the Red Barn. The murder was notorious in the 19th century and retained a hold on popular imagination throughout the country. Details of the events in 1827 are included in a booklet obtainable from the Polstead Community Shop, which is volunteer-run and one of the oldest of its kind in Suffolk.

The Cock Inn

From its prominent position on Polstead Green, the 17th-century Cock Inn – a popular walking pub – looks out over the rest of the village. The attractive garden, complete with tables and parasols, is an inviting place to eat and drink in warm weather. Inside, the bar lounge has scrubbed tables, exposed brick walls and timber beams. Meals may be taken there or in the Victorian style restaurant extension. Displayed on a wall are rosettes awarded to the Cock by the AA for culinary excellence. The comprehensive menu offers fresh fish, meat and vegetable dishes, curries and tagliatelle, also salads, ploughman's and filled jacket potatoes. An unusual item, which is immensely popular, is the 'Suffolk Huffer' – large white baps served with a choice of 30 plus fillings – which can be eaten here or taken away. Special three-course lunches for senior citizens are also available. The real ales on offer include Adnams and a guest beer that is changed monthly. Kronenbourg and Carlsberg lagers and Guinness are served too. Chalked up on a blackboard are details of selected malt whiskeys. Well-behaved children are welcome in the garden and restaurant; dogs are allowed in the bar area only. The Cock is open every day except Mondays. Telephone: 01206 263150.

The Walk

① With the village shop in front, turn right to join Heath Road. After about 300 yards, turn left by a fingerpost and walk towards the wood ahead of you. Descend the steepish bank and turn right at the

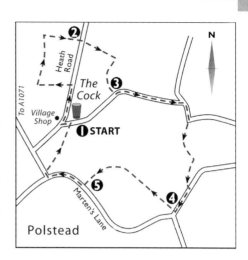

bottom. Follow a well-defined path for about 250 yards and then take a right fork to climb up the slope. Turn left at the top and continue round the headland to a stile. Cross the latter and continue to join Heath Road again.

② Turn left and carry on along the road for about 75 yards. Turn right onto a field edge path and continue with a hedge on the left. When you reach a crossway of paths, turn right to join a RUPP (road used as a public path). Continue ahead on what looks like an old earth lane to arrive at a minor road. For a short cut back to the pub, turn right.

③ For the full route, turn left and pass Rockalls Lodge just ahead. Carry on to the next road junction and bear right. Just where the road bends left, turn right onto an unmarked track. Follow the track and turn left at the bottom to join a sunken earth lane. Eventually emerge onto the road and turn right. With a road junction further ahead, turn right through a hedge gap and cross a stile.

Paddocks passed en route

④ Go downhill over pasture beside a paddock fence. At the bottom, cross three stiles in quick succession. Keep to the left of a barn and stay on the path – known as the Red Barn Path – where it shortly runs between pasture and a belt of woodland. Stay on the path to finally reach a corner. Cross a stile, bear left and stay close to the left edge to meet a lane at the top.

⑤ Turn right and proceed down Marten's Lane with Maria Marten's cottage standing on the right. At Bells Corner, carry straight on and shortly turn right by a fingerpost to join a rising path that finally brings you back to your start point.

PLACES OF INTEREST NEARBY
Hadleigh Guildhall is a fine medieval timber-framed building consisting of three halls, one with a crown post. There are organised tours from time to time. Standing nearby is the **historic church of St Mary** and the **Deanery Tower**. The town also contains some other interesting buildings. Telephone: 01473 827752 for details about the Guildhall.

Hadleigh
The Ram

MAP: OS EXPLORER 196 (GR 024424)   **WALK 9**   **DISTANCE:** 2½ MILES

DIRECTIONS TO START: HADLEIGH IS 9 MILES WEST OF IPSWICH AND CAN BE APPROACHED BY THE A1071, AND FROM SUDBURY BY THE A134/A1071. FROM THE HIGH STREET TURN INTO DUKE STREET AND THEN TO TOPPESFIELD BRIDGE CAR PARK. **PARKING:** THE (FREE) TOPPESFIELD BRIDGE CAR PARK, THREE MINUTES' WALK AWAY. ALTERNATIVELY, THERE IS A PAY AND DISPLAY CAR PARK NEXT TO THE PUB.

During the 15th and early 16th centuries, Hadleigh grew rich from the manufacture of wool cloth. Some of its wealth can be seen in many of the fine medieval buildings that survive today. Just around the corner from the Ram, you'll find the brick Deanery Tower, built in 1495; Standing alongside it is St Mary's church, with its soaring spire and across the way stands the impressive Grade I listed Guildhall, which has been put to several uses during its 600 years, including a cloth hall, a workhouse and, nowadays, it's the town council. This stroll climbs to high ground, where a grand view of the town is possible, and finishes along a delightful stretch of riverside and woodland.

The Ram

You'll find the Ram tucked away in a street by the market place, just off the High Street. At one time the pub must have been handy for the former cattle and livestock markets held in the town. Nowadays it is well patronised by locals and long-standing customers who come into the town for shopping. Expect to find excellent, good value food here – little wonder there are few tables vacant, especially at peak times. Most meals are taken in the bar area, and, during the warmer weather, you can eat outside on picnic tables in a raised courtyard. Set meals include the likes of crispy battered cod, seafood platter, fisherman's pie, cooked chicken breast, shepherd's pie, sausage and mash and meat lasagne. There is also a selection of vegetarian meals on offer. For something lighter, the Ram does sandwiches and filled jacket potatoes. Drinks include Greene King IPA and Abbot plus other real ales. The pub is open all day, every day. It's a good idea to phone in advance to reserve a table. Telephone: 01473 822171.

The Walk

① From outside the Ram, bear left in front of the pay and display car park and follow the road round to Duke Street. Turn right here and go over Toppesfield Bridge in front. With the Toppesfield Bridge car park on the right, carry on straight ahead on a concreted path. Pass the entrance to Holbecks Park beside a cattle grid and now carry on along a farm track.

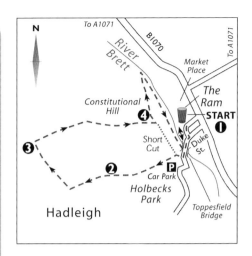

② Pass an isolated house and buildings on the right and stay on the track, which soon starts to climb quite sharply. Follow the track to the top end and turn right by a green circular walk sign. Continue ahead on a very broad grassy path. If you wish to visit the lovely area around Kersey Vale, to the west, this path links with others to take you there. From gaps in the hedgerow you may catch a view of the grey spire of Hadleigh church and part of the town nestling in the valley below.

PLACES OF INTEREST NEARBY

In addition to the many buildings of interest in **Hadleigh** itself, **Gainsborough's House** at Sudbury, 11 miles west of Hadleigh, is the birthplace of Thomas Gainsborough (1727-1788), one of England's greatest painters. It is now open as an art gallery and museum, with more of his paintings and prints on display here than anywhere else in the world. The house has a collection of over 2,000 items but not all are on show. Telephone: 01787 372958.

Hadleigh's guildhall

③ Keep forward to shortly turn right by a sign marked 'Constitutional Hill'. Continue on a field edge path with a hedge on the left, which takes you back towards the town. At the boundary enter the adjoining field, with an undulating path in front. At the bottom, fork right to descend over some rough grassland. Skirt an area of woodland on the left and ignore a crossway of paths. Stay on the path if you wish to return to the car park.

④ Otherwise, turn left where the path curves right and continue ahead to shortly reach an entrance to a caravan club on the left. Turn right here to join the Hadleigh Riverside Walk. Stay beside the river on a well-defined path as it winds its way through woodland. When you reach Toppesfield Bridge, retrace your steps to your point of departure.

Bildeston
The Red Lion

DIRECTIONS TO START: BILDESTON LIES ON THE B1115 STOWMARKET-HADLEIGH ROAD. THE RED LION IS SITUATED IN THE HIGH STREET, NEXT DOOR TO THE LOCAL HEALTH CENTRE. **PARKING:** PARK IN THE PUB YARD OR ON THE MARKET PLACE.

Bildeston has a market place without a market and a church half a mile away from the centre, but the reasons for this are clear when one delves into the village's history. A small community once lived beside the church, the inhabitants moving to the river valley at some point during the 13th century, possibly because of the cloth trade, which later brought prosperity to Bildeston. The market declined during the 18th century, when traders were attracted to a bigger and better market at nearby Hadleigh. The village has many fine half-timbered houses, some dating from the middle of the 15th century. This attractive walk takes you beside fields and woodland to some of the highest ground in Suffolk, where Wattisham Airfield, home to army helicopters, can be seen.

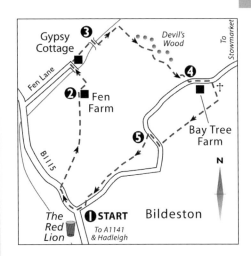

The Red Lion

This pub stands almost in the centre of the village and has recently undergone a programme of complete refurbishment. Walkers are particularly welcome here. The comprehensive menu contains plenty of traditional pub nosh. Dishes include curry, lasagne, steaks, fish, shepherd's pie and Sunday roasts. There are also lite bites and sandwiches available, plus a take-away menu. Food may be eaten in a revamped bar area or in the restaurant. Drinks currently served include Greene King favourites and Woodforde's Wherry. Order your meal before the walk and it will be ready on your return. The pub is open on Tuesday, Wednesday and Thursday from 12 noon to 2.30 pm and from 5 pm to 11 pm; on Friday and Saturday from 11.30 am to 1 am; and on Sunday from 12 noon to 10 pm. Please note it is closed all day Monday. Telephone: 01449 740476.

The Walk

① Walk along the High Street on a footway, passing the market place and Wattisham Road. Just past the last house, where the road bends left, turn right onto a field edged path. Continue with the hedge on the right along an ascending path. Shortly, cross a ditch and enter the adjoining field.

② Stay on the well-defined path as it curves left and right. Just after it descends slightly, turn right over a sleeper bridge and head towards Fen Farm in front. Pass the farm on the right and keep going ahead to reach Fen Lane where you turn left. At the far end swing right into another field and pass Gypsy Cottage immediately on the right. Carry on to the field corner and turn right into a thicket. Keep straight ahead and exit the thicket by a bridge and some steps in the bank.

③ Turn left and maintain direction for about 400 yards. Swing left and right to continue on a broad stony track. Take the next turning right, pass through a short area of scrub and turn left the other side. Pass beside a row of conifer trees and follow the field edge to the corner to climb up the left side. At the top, skirt the length of Devil's Wood along a cart track to

PLACES OF INTEREST NEARBY

Lavenham's **Guildhall of Corpus Christi** is a superb 16th-century Tudor timber-framed house, with a delightful garden. Inside there are exhibitions on local history, including a fascinating display of 700 years of the medieval woollen cloth trade. The building also contains a restored 19th-century parish lock-up and mortuary. Lavenham is reached on the A1141 west of Bildeston. Telephone: 01787 247646.

Duke Street, Bildeston

eventually reach a road. For the 3-mile option, turn right, pass some cottages and, in another 400 yards, turn right beside a footpath sign onto a field edge path.

④ For the full route, turn left and just after reaching a 30 mph restriction sign, turn right onto a field edged path. Turn right over a shallow ditch at the boundary and continue on a cart track. Swing right to enter another field and continue straight ahead to reach a road. Turn right here and, in 150 yards, turn left onto another field edged path.

⑤ Stay on the descending path through successive fields, passing over the driveway to 'Bentons'. Later pass between a laurel hedge and a plantation of trees. Stay on the path to finally reach Tasker Farmyard. Turn right to join Wattisham Road and go left at the T-junction. The Red Lion is 150 yards past the market place on the right.

Great Finborough
The Chestnut Horse

MAP: OS EXPLORER 211 (GR 014577)   **WALK 11**   DISTANCE: 5 MILES

DIRECTIONS TO START: TAKE THE B1115 ROAD FROM EITHER STOWMARKET OR BILDESTON. THE CHESTNUT HORSE STANDS IN THE CENTRE OF GREAT FINBOROUGH VILLAGE. **PARKING:** THERE IS ROOM TO PARK AT THE SIDE AND REAR OF THE PUB.

Positioned in the village centre, the Chestnut Horse is ideally placed for strolls around Finborough Park and Buxhall Vale. On this walk, you'll discover a couple of delightful green lanes, with their thick hedgerows still intact, reminiscent perhaps of rural Suffolk long before the advent of 'prairie farming'. Under the Countryside Stewardship Scheme, an enlightened landowner has left a green area for all to enjoy. Included in the scheme is some attractive meadowland, which is carpeted with wild flowers in the early summer months. The tall spire of St Andrew's church, shaped like a sharpened pencil or maybe a space rocket, dominates the skyline for miles around and acts as a useful landmark.

The Chestnut Horse

You are assured of a warm welcome at this unpretentious country pub. Here you can relax in a longish bar area, have a round of darts perhaps or join in banter with the locals. You might learn something about the annual (usually Easter Monday) Race of the Bogmen, which finishes here. Details listing the background to this not too serious event hang on a wall. The Chestnut Horse was a former farmhouse and opened for business as a pub in 1876. From a typical menu you can choose from dishes such as cod and chips, cheese and broccoli bake and a real favourite here, steak and ale pie, also sandwiches, baguettes and jacket potatoes with various fillings. Sunday roasts are also extremely popular. Desserts include spotted dick, lemon meringue cake and treacle pudding. For drinks there is a range of Greene King ales and draught Guinness. Food may be eaten in a non-smoking area separated from the bar. If you fancy sitting outside, there are tables and parasols in front of the building. Children and dogs are welcome. The pub is open seven days a week during normal licensing hours. Telephone: 01449 612298.

The Walk

① Cross the road from the pub and turn left. Just before reaching the village shop in front, turn right over a stile into pasture. Cross the pasture and aim towards a partially-hidden kissing gate positioned in the boundary hedge in front. Take a downhiill path over the crest of a hill, cross a bridge at the bottom and maintain direction. The path leads towards an electricity pole on the left

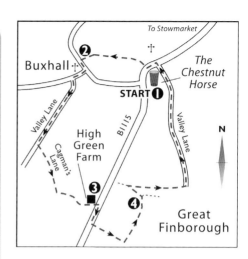

and shortly meets another path going left and right. Turn left here and go past the pole.

② Head in the direction of Buxhall church in front. At the boundary, turn left on to a minor road and shortly turn right by the village sign to join Brettenham Road. Take the next left turn into Valley Lane and continue along a surfaced stretch for about another 800 yards. Just before reaching the isolated Orchard Cottage, turn left onto a byway known as 'Cagman's Lane'. At the far end, follow the path as it curves left to finally reach a hedge. Bear right and left here and stay on the path, which finally

PLACES OF INTEREST NEARBY

The **Museum of East Anglian Life** in Stowmarket houses a variety of collections appertaining mainly to rural life. Attractions include a working windmill, a tithe barn and re-created rooms depicting life during Victorian times and the 1950s. There are also displays of farming, craft workshops and industry, along with Suffolk Punch horses and rare breeds of cattle, pigs and sheep. Telephone: 01449 612229.

Buxhall's attractive village sign

brings you to High Green Farm and the B1115.

③ Turn right and walk beside the road for about 25 yards before turning left into City Lane. Follow the latter until it peters out and then bear left with a hedge on the left. Soon you will join a lovely green lane, with mature hedgerows either side. Carry on ahead for about 25 yards and, just beyond a dead oak tree, where the path bears right, break left through a hedge gap.

④ Turn right, stay beside the field edge and shortly go left through an attractive meadow setting. As you walk up the slope opposite, look for a stile at the top with the spire of Finborough church standing some distance beyond it. Turn right over the stile and stay on a descending field edge path to reach another Valley Lane. At the bottom, turn left and follow the surfaced lane back to the junction with the B1115. Turn left and the Chestnut Horse is just around the corner.

Rickinghall
The Bell Inn

DIRECTIONS TO START: RICKINGHALL LIES 6 MILES WEST OF DISS. LEAVE THE A143 AT THE TURN-OFF FOR BOTESDALE AND RICKINGHALL TO ENTER THE STREET. THE BELL IS SITUATED IN THE VILLAGE CENTRE. **PARKING:** TO THE SIDE AND REAR OF THE PUB.

This walk was supposed to start from Botesdale, a large village situated towards the Norfolk border. No problem, a large Botesdale village sign stands beside the road a few yards away from the local post office. However, mine host at the Bell later tells me that his pub, located almost opposite the above mentioned sign and intended start point of the walk, is in fact geographically part of Rickinghall. Just where one village starts and the other finishes has been a source of puzzlement to locals for many a year. But this doesn't detract from an easy and pleasant stroll. The villages straddle an old coaching route. According to *White's Directory of Suffolk (1844)* 'coaches pass eight times a day to Norwich, Bury St Edmunds and London'. Georgian and Victorian houses line the main street, high ground along the way provides a scenic view of the surrounding countryside.

The Bell Inn

Standing beside the village street, the Bell was formerly a 17th-century coaching inn, serving the needs of travellers in terms of food, drink, accommodation and the stabling of horses. Nowadays, it still offers accommodation and refreshment to people from far and wide. Casual visitors, such as walkers, are also welcomed and catered for. Inside the bar lounge partially exposed brick walls, old beams, brasses and an inglenook fireplace co-exist with modern comforts. Displayed on the walls are pictures of farming scenes in the local area, and a couple of humorous facsimile documents describe innkeeping rules and regulations pertaining to the 18th century. Upholstered seating and a carpeted floor help to create a cosy ambience. A pool table is available for patrons' use. A wide-ranging snack menu, which often changes, includes all day breakfasts, baguettes, jacket potatoes and salad items. The main menu offers the likes of sirloin and rump steak, lamb steak, chicken goujons, chicken breast, pasta, scampi and chef's specials. There is also a varied choice of desserts plus a good selection of beers and lagers. Meals may be eaten in the spacious bar lounge or in the small restaurant. Outside there is a patio garden to enjoy. Children and dogs are allowed if accompanied by an adult. The pub is open from 11 am to 3 pm Monday to Thursday, and from 11 am to 11 pm Friday, Saturday and Sunday. Telephone: 01379 898445.

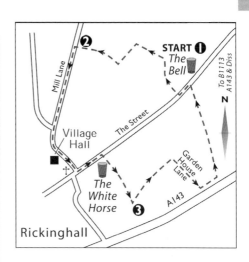

The Walk

① Leave the Bell and turn right along the footway, passing Botesdale post office on the other side of the road. In another 20 yards, turn right beside a footpath sign to join a partially surfaced path, which gently descends between wooden fences. At the bottom, cross a footbridge and follow the path right. Continue on a narrow path beside lowland meadows. Turn left over a brick bridge and continue to the far end of a grass and gravel path. Bear left, stay on the path and curve right just before meeting a large oak tree. Carry on beside the field edge to meet a quiet lane at the top.

② Turn left here and follow Mill Lane for about another 600 yards. Turn left again to join the Hinderclay (to the right) road and pass the village hall on the right. Just after passing St Mary's church turn left into the main street. Cross the road when you are level with the White Horse pub to locate and join a grassy path. Continue up the rising path which gives excellent views all round. Carry on to reach a fingerpost and turn left.

Suffolk in late summer

③ Keep forward with a hedge on the right and shortly pass between a pair of electricity poles. Go through a green area and afterwards walk beside an enclosed hedge. Turn right and continue along a wide track, which takes you to the bypass road ahead. Go left beside a metal gate, walk parallel with the road for 75 yards and pass under power lines. Shortly turn left again to take a path heading back towards the village. At the field boundary, pass a property called Bunny Hollow and maintain direction downhill to meet the street at the bottom. Turn right and the Bell is just across the road.

PLACES OF INTEREST NEARBY
Bressingham Steam Museum and Gardens, 2½ miles west of Diss on the A1066, offer something for everyone. A narrow gauge railway takes visitors for rides around the nursery grounds. Ex-British Rail steam engines can be viewed at close quarters. On display elsewhere is a Dad's Army Exhibition, based on the BBC TV series. Close by are the world-renowned gardens created by Alan and Adrian Bloom. Telephone: 01379 686900.

Thornham Magna
The Four Horseshoes

MAP: OS EXPLORER 230 AND 211 (GR 104707) | **WALK 13** | **DISTANCE:** 3½ MILES

DIRECTIONS TO START: LEAVE THE A140 NORWICH-IPSWICH ROAD AT THE TURN-OFF FOR WICKHAM SKEITH BESIDE THE STOKE ASH WHITE HORSE PUB. FOLLOW THE WICKHAM ROAD TO REACH THE FOUR HORSESHOES ON THE RIGHT. **PARKING:** THERE IS PLENTY OF SPACE IN A CAR PARK ACROSS THE ROAD IN FRONT OF THE PUB.

On this pleasant walk in an un-crowded part of Suffolk you are unlikely to encounter too many people, save for farmworkers and fellow walkers perhaps. The route progresses through part of Thornham Magna village beside field edge paths, woodland and along quiet country lanes. Some of the paths walked are courtesy of the nearby Thornham Estate, owned by the Henniker family since 1756. The present Lord and Lady Henniker opened up the estate for educational and recreational purposes and to provide local employment. Scattered along the way you will discover a number of thatched cottages, some secluded and decorated with the traditional Suffolk pink wash. The latter part of the stroll takes you over a long stretch of pasture beside the River Dove as it meanders its way through the rural landscape. In parts the Dove is little more than a shallow stream, tending to dry up during periods of prolonged drought.

The Four Horseshoes

Turn off the traffic-congested A140 and after a short while you reach the relative peace and quietness of Thornham Magna. The Four Horseshoes is an attractive pub standing beside the village crossroads. One of the first things you will notice about this restored 12th-century building is its impressive thatched roof, much in keeping with other properties found in the village. Step inside the spacious bar lounge and you are given a warm welcome. The décor consists of old farm tools and pictures of the countryside, along with fruit machines, piped music and large wintertime log fires. An unusual feature is a wishing well, complete with a rope and bucket. Apparently this once stood outside but when an extension was built, it was decided to leave the well in situ and build round it. Among the bar snacks, you are likely to find jacket potatoes, ploughman's and sandwiches. Chef's specials include dishes such as grilled sea bass, braised lamb shank and traditional fish and chips. Meat and game pies are particular favourites here. Food may be eaten in the bar lounge or in the no-smoking restaurant. Real ales on offer include Greene King IPA and Abbot and Morland Old Speckled Hen. The pub is open for food seven days a week. Children and dogs are welcome. Telephone: 01379 678777.

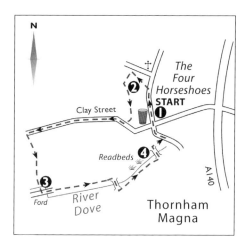

The Walk

① From the car park, cross the road and pass the pub on the left. Continue ahead until you reach the Forge Workshops and a red telephone box. Turn left onto a field edge path, with a hedge on the right. Maintain direction and shortly turn left to join a track (Gull Lane). Pass a secluded cottage on the right and pass another one at the end of the lane. Carry straight on up some steps in the bank to skirt a copse on the right.

② Continue down the soon descending track to eventually reach a ford over the River Dove. If the ford is impassable, turn left up a bank and take the narrow path. At the road junction ahead turn left to follow the Thornham road. Shortly pass through a kissing gate on the right and carry on beside the riverbank. Later, enter some more pasture and cross the river by a concrete bridge with a metal handrail. Follow the opposite bank to a substantial wooden gate and cross the stile beside it.

③ Continue down the soon descending track to eventually reach a ford over the River Dove. If the ford is impassable, turn left up a bank and take a narrow path. At the road junction turn left, cross a road bridge and swing right and left onto a concrete hard standing. Climb the stile in

The River Dove wending its way through pastures

front and carry on beside the riverbank. Later, enter some more pasture and cross the river by a concrete bridge with a metal handrail. Follow the opposite bank to a substantial wooden gate and cross a stile beside it.

④ Go past some reedbeds and soon turn left to take the 'short way' as painted in red on a fence. Cross the river once more and continue on a narrow path beside a barbed wire fence. Turn left when you meet Water Lane, and follow it to reach the crossroads, with the pub appearing in front.

PLACES OF INTEREST NEARBY

If you drive northwards up the A140 you can visit the historic town and former borough of **Eye** to climb to the top of the Norman castle ruins, from where there is a bird's view of the original town layout shaped like an island – 'Eye' is derived from the Saxon word for island. The church of St Peter and St Paul with its impressive 100 ft tower is also worth a visit. Telephone Mid Suffolk Tourist Information Centre: 01449 676800.

Stowupland
The Crown

MAP: OS EXPLORER 211 (GR 069598)   **WALK 14**   **DISTANCE:** 3½ MILES

DIRECTIONS TO START: LEAVE THE A14 AT STOWMARKET AND TAKE THE A1120 TO NEARBY STOWUPLAND. THE CROWN IS ON THE LEFT JUST AFTER PASSING THE OPEN SPACE OF THORNEY GREEN. **PARKING:** LIMITED PARKING IN FRONT OF PUB. IF FULL, TRY THE VILLAGE HALL NEXT DOOR IF NOT IN USE.

Stowupland is a scattered parish, with a couple of pubs, a high school and primary school, a post office and general stores and a large open space known as Thorney Green. Sections of the green extend through the centre of the village, where it is surrounded by attractive cottages. The stroll itself explores a stretch of unspoilt countryside in central Suffolk. Part of the way is walked along the Mid Suffolk Path, which links Hoxne in the north with Stowmarket in the south. The route is marked with a poppy emblem, reflecting the wild poppies that can be found growing in nearby fields during the summer months. After a mile or so, you reach some high ground, which gives a superb panoramic view of the immediate countryside set deep in a valley. The source of the infant River Gipping is not far away. As yet unpolluted, it slowly makes its way to Stowmarket and thence to Ipswich, where it becomes the Orwell before finally flowing into the North Sea.

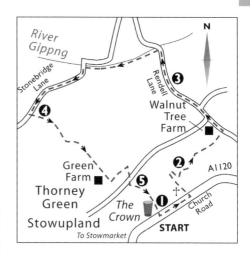

The Crown

This thatched pub is well over 500 years old and overseas visitors will find it the quintessential Suffolk inn, with its timber beams decorated with horse brasses, low ceilings, wooden tables and benches. However, a fruit machine, piped music and a wide screen television are among a few concessions to modernism in an otherwise traditional pub atmosphere. If you require something light to eat, the Crown does a variety of sandwiches, also 'snack attacks' – dishes such as soup of the day, egg, sausage, chips and beans and a quarter pound burger with relish. In the small restaurant just off the bar area, you can choose from a wide-ranging menu, including battered cod and haddock, lasagne, seafood platter, chicken nuggets and home-made steak and kidney pie. To complement the food there are Greene King favourites and other real ales. Outside, the large beer garden has various amusements to keep the children happy. The pub is open seven days a week but no food is served on Monday. Telephone: 01449 674571.

The Walk

① Turn left into Church Road and shortly go left again onto a tarmac path, which runs between Holy Trinity church and the primary school. Follow the path, with a playing field on either side. Turn right at the far end and stay on a narrow path to skirt the playing field before turning left over a footbridge in the corner.

② Take a field edge path to enter an area of rough grassland further ahead. Cross diagonally to the far left-hand corner. Go left through a gateway and quickly turn right over a footbridge. Follow a field edge path and finally leave the field beside an electricity pylon. Turn left to join Rendell Lane and shortly pass Walnut Tree Farm. Ignore later turnings to Stowmarket, Gipping and Mendlesham.

③ Admire the superb views before gradually descending a long hill. At the bottom, turn left onto a field edge path. Stay on the path until you eventually reach a bridge with some railings. Turn left here to join Stonebridge Lane. Carry on for another 500 yards and turn left by a fingerpost onto a grassy farm track, with a hedge on the left.

④ Continue on the rising track, which later becomes rutted, and cross a stile by a gate. At the top end veer left to cross a stile in the corner of a hedge. Maintain direction and shortly pass through a small metal gate. Bear left when you reach Green Farm buildings ahead to soon emerge at Thorney Green. Turn left and follow the gravel path to the next corner,

Thorney Green, Stowupland

where it curves right by some bungalows. Keep skirting the Green to arrive at Thorney Green Road.

⑤ Turn right and a few yards later go left by a phone box to reach an open area of grass. Follow the right-hand hedge to a corner. Turn left to join a school access drive and continue to the junction with Church Road. Turn right and the Crown is just beside you.

PLACES OF INTEREST NEARBY
The only railway museum in Suffolk can be found on a green site at the former **Brockford station**, near the track bed of the former Mid-Suffolk Light Railway. This is just south of Wetheringsett and is reached from the A140 north-east of Stowupland. A typical Mid-Suffolk station has been created along with the preservation of rolling stock, original buildings and artefacts. Occasional steam days are held during the season. Telephone: 01449 766899.

Needham Market
The Lion

DISTANCE TO START: LEAVE THE A14 BURY ST EDMUNDS TO IPSWICH ROAD AT THE
A140 BEACON HILL INTERCHANGE AND FOLLOW THE B1078 TO NEEDHAM MARKET.
THE LION LIES BESIDE THE B1113 AT THE EASTERN SIDE OF THE TOWN.
PARKING: THERE IS A LARGE CAR PARK BESIDE THE PUB.

You soon escape the noise of traffic as you head along grassy paths to arrive at the hamlet of Darmsden. On high ground near the isolated church of St Andrew you are compensated with sense of relative peace and tranquillity. Here, you can obtain sweeping views across a length of the Gipping valley and the surrounding countryside. Nearby are picturesque cottages and gardens. The valley is rich in mineral deposits, providing sand and gravel for the road and house building industries. Where extraction has been exhausted, pits have been flooded to provide valuable wildlife habitats and recreation for anglers. Flocks of Canada geese, moorhens and coots frequent the pits, and occasionally there is the sighting of a kingfisher, grey heron or great crested grebe. Needham Lake, another former gravel pit, is a popular attraction, especially during the summer months. Activities include fishing, sailing model boats and exploring a small nature reserve.

The Lion

This is one of the most popular pubs in the area. Situated on the Ipswich road, it is not, strictly speaking, in Needham Market but in the adjoining parish of Barking – according to a local book entitled *Needham Market Pubs*, it's thought that the official name change from Barking Lion to Needham Lion took place around 1923 during the Cobbold (local brewers) 200th anniversary celebrations. Prior to the 1960s the landlord used to disappear down into the cellar to draw beer direct from the barrel, or wood as it was known. After a complete refurbishment, food and drinks are nowadays served in a relaxed atmosphere on two floor levels. Memories of the original pub and its exterior can be found in photographs hanging on the walls. The menu contains a little bit of everything, including generous portion of dishes such as seafood platter, traditional roasts, steak and ale pie, lasagne, gammon steaks and scampi, also sandwiches, ploughman's and salads. On fine days, food can be eaten outside on tables in a terraced patio garden where there is also an amusement area to occupy the children. Drinks on offer include a wide selection of real ales and cask beers. If you wish, you can order your choice of meal before you start walking and it will be ready for you on your return. Telephone: 01449 720849.

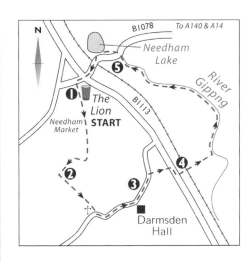

The Walk

① Turn left out of the car park and proceed up Grinstead Hill. In about 75 yards, turn left to join a rising path. Stay on the leafy path, passing a quarry on the left before arriving in open countryside. Keep straight ahead on a broad path running between two fields. At the boundary ignore a path gong left and bear right, shortly accompanied by a hedge. Your path now bends right, with the remnants of a ditch on the left. Turn left when you reach a marker post and after 250 yards turn left again on to a cart track.

② Go down a valley and up the other side to pass the lonely church of St Andrew at the top. The track now gives way to a surfaced lane, which shortly bears left. Continue along the gently descending lane to eventually pass Darmsden Hall on the right.

③ Maintain direction and just after the lane starts to descend again, bear right into a wooded thicket by a fingerpost. Exit the thicket into an arable field and continue downwards to meet the B1113 at the bottom. Cross the road, with care, and turn right. Continue on a footway for about 100 yards and then turn left through an access gate for lorries.

Needham Lake

④ Continue straight ahead and go over a stile to cross a railway line. Cross another stile and carry on along a well-defined path over some set-aside land. Turn left at the far end to join the Gipping Valley River Path. Stay on the path as it passes through an area of lowland meadows.

⑤ Finally leave the path by a kissing gate and turn sharp right onto the B1078. Go forward a few paces, and cross the road to the entrance opposite, which brings you to Needham Lake. Go over an arched bridge and continue, with the lake on the right. Proceed through the main entrance, turn right and go under the railway bridge. Continue on a footway for a further 75 yards and cross the road to enter a small housing estate. Keep veering left to eventually reach Lion Lane. Turn right here and the Lion is just in front of you.

> **PLACES OF INTEREST NEARBY**
> **Baylham Rare Breeds Farm**, just off the B1113 to the south of Needham Market, contains breeding groups of rare cattle, sheep, pigs and poultry. The aim is to help maintain the national pool of endangered rare breeds. Children can come into contact with healthy and contented animals. The farm is on part of the Roman site of Combretevium, which included two Roman forts and a large civil settlement. Telephone: 01473 830264.

Bramford
The Cock

DIRECTIONS TO START: LEAVE THE A14 AT CLAYDON, NORTH OF IPSWICH, AND TAKE THE B1113. FOLLOW THE ROAD SIGNS TO BRAMFORD AND LOCATE THE COCK IN BRAMFORD STREET. **PARKING:** PARK AT THE SIDE OR REAR OF THE PUB.

Fronting the River Gipping are flood plain grasslands, well used by walkers and anglers. On the opposite bank is a picturesque view of St Mary's church, with its grand tower and spire. This stretch of river path was used by horses in the early 19th century to tow barges along the Gipping Navigation between Ipswich and Stowmarket. The path links Bramford to the next village of Sproughton, where water from the Gipping was harnessed to power the mill, now seen in a dilapidated condition. The Grindle, a narrow lane with a stream running alongside, acts as an ancient boundary, not just between the parishes of Bramford and Sproughton, but also between the Hundreds of Bosmere and Samford. Further on, the high ground gives sweeping views over the immediate countryside and beyond.

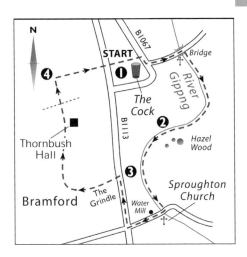

The Cock

Step down from the pavement and you may experience that sinking feeling as you enter the bar lounge. It's all due to the pavement, which has been built up over successive centuries, making the floor appear lower. When people started to grow taller, apparently, rather than raise the roof, the floor was dug out and lowered – or so the story goes. The Cock, which dates from the early 17th century, retains many of its original beams, with some thought to have come from the timber of old barges. Chalked up on boards inside are details of bar snacks and a wide variety of main courses such as fish, steaks, lasagne, traditional roasts and rice dishes. A large selection of desserts is also available. Beers and ales include Flowers, Tetley's, Guinness and Carlsberg lager. Food may be eaten in the bar area or in the adjoining conservatory, which acts as a restaurant. The Cock takes pride in serving freshly cooked food and there may be delays during busy periods. Well-behaved children and dogs (bar only) are welcome. The pub is open seven days a week and food is available every lunchtime from Monday to Saturday and on Saturday evening but the kitchen is closed all day on Sunday. Booking is advised for meals, especially on Saturday. Telephone: 01473 747939.

The Walk

① Leave the car park, turn right and follow the B1067 as it curves left along Ship Lane. Go past an entrance to the church and reach a bridge over the River Gipping. Turn right down some steps and make for the riverside. Turn left and walk beside the Gipping through some water meadows. Stay beside the river as it meanders its way towards Ipswich. After about 800 yards you can make a detour into Hazel Wood if you wish.

② Soon the river passes through stretches of lowland. When you finally reach Sproughton village with the dilapidated mill on the right, leave the river, go up some steps and turn right at the top onto the road. With All Saints' church on the left, make your way up Lower Street, passing the former village lock up and the post office. At the road junction ahead, turn right to join the B1113. Continue

PLACES OF INTEREST NEARBY

Christchurch Mansion in Ipswich is a historic 16th-century property set in beautiful parkland. Period rooms represented include a sumptuous Georgian saloon as well as a more humble Victorian wing with its display of children's toys and doll's houses. The house also includes paintings by Gainsborough, Constable and other Suffolk artists. Telephone: 01473 433554.

Bramford's village sign

along the footway for about 300 yards to reach the Bramford boundary signpost.

③ Cross the road and make your way up The Grindle, a gently rising narrow lane. When you reach the far end – just past Grindle Farm – turn right. Go forward over a grassy area and veer slightly right to join a farm track. Continue along the track, which brings you up to Thornbush Hall. Bear left to skirt some farm buildings, then veer right and shortly take a rising stony path with a hedge on the right.

④ Where the track curves left at the top, turn right to follow a grassy path, which separates two fields. At the field boundary, cross the B1113, with care, and carry straight on. Skirt a school playing field on the right and turn right when you finally reach Bramford Street. The Cock is a few paces further.

East Bergholt
The Red Lion

MAP: OS EXPLORER 196 (GR 069346) — **WALK 17** — **DISTANCE:** 4 MILES

DIRECTIONS TO START: LEAVE THE A12 AT THE EAST BERGHOLT TURN OFF AND FOLLOW THE B1070, HADLEIGH ROAD, TO THE VILLAGE CENTRE.
PARKING: DUE TO LIMITED PARKING OUTSIDE THE PUB, IT'S BEST TO PARK IN THE ADJACENT FREE (AT TIME OF WRITING) PUBLIC CAR PARK.

This lovely walk takes you by way of meadow, riverside, valley and farmland to Dedham Vale, just over the county border into Essex. The idyllic scene, within an area of outstanding natural beauty, includes the sight of soaring church towers and cattle grazing in lush pasture. The route passes through countryside known nowadays as Constable country, an area immortalised by England's greatest landscape painter, John Constable (1776-1837), who grew up in East Bergholt where his father owned Flatford Mill. He frequently returned to his roots, seeking inspiration for his later paintings. A plaque marks the spot of Constable's studio (1802) just as you turn into Cemetery Lane. The natural beauty still draws artists from a wide area and many can be seen painting and sketching in the open air just as Constable did.

The Red Lion

There has been a pub on this site for well over 200 years and possibly longer, during which time a number of alterations have taken place. Well placed in the village centre near the local post office and stores, the Red Lion is popular with walkers who wish to explore the local area. The hamlet of Flatford, Constable Country and Dedham Vale can all be easily accessed from here. The extensive menu at the Red Lion includes daily specials as well as chicken and mushroom pie, lamb stew, seafood platter, vegetable curry and home-cooked ham and chips. Light bites such as sandwiches with delicious fillings are also served. Desserts include cheesecakes, apple pie, sorbets and ice cream. There is also a children's menu. If you want to book your meal before you leave on your walk, it will be ready when you return. The bar offers a wide variety of wines and spirits with a good selection of real ales and beers. Morning tea and coffee are also available. Drinks and meals may be taken in the well-furnished bar lounge, the family restaurant or in the beer garden. Dogs are allowed only in the public bar. Food is available daily except for Sunday evenings and booking is advisable at busy times. Telephone: 01206 298332.

The Walk

① From the pub, bear right and pass the post office to join Cemetery Lane. At the far end, continue downhill on a grassy path. Cross a road and carry on uphill in the field opposite. Go through a gate and continue on a field edge path to reach a junction of

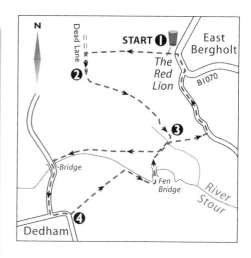

paths. Turn left along Dead Lane, a sunken path.

② Turn left at the bottom and walk with a hedge on the right and later between hedgerows. Shortly turn right and left as waymarked to cross a stile followed by a timber bridge. Do not cross a stile on the right but bear left through a small wood and shortly cross a stile into a field. Keep beside a hedge on the right and soon cross a stile in the hedge. Maintain direction, with a hedge now on the left, and finally reach a meadow. Cross a stile in the corner and turn right into Fen Lane.

③ Follow the latter round and cross a cart track over water. In about another 100 yards, turn half right by a footpath sign which takes you to a broad meadow by the River Stour and eventually up some steps in a bank to reach Dedham. Turn left onto the road and left again at the next T-junction. Just past the Art and Craft Centre, where the road bears right, turn left along a gravel track signed 'Public Footpath to Flatford'.

The cage containing the church bells of East Bergholt

④ Ignore a National Trust footpath and carry on ahead. Pass through two metal kissing gates to reach a broad meadow. Cross roughly diagonally to reach the Stour. Follow the riverbank to the right to cross Fen Bridge. Continue along Fen Lane to where you walked earlier and cross the wooden cart bridge. Shortly, instead of going left, carry straight on to climb a grassy hill. At the top, cross the road, climb a low bank and turn left along a path which runs parallel to the road. When the path ends, continue along the road to reach a T-junction. Turn left towards the village centre and car park.

PLACES OF INTEREST NEARBY

Bridge Cottage in nearby Flatford is a 16th-century thatched property belonging to the National Trust. Inside there is a free exhibition about John Constable and his paintings, which includes facsimile copies of his sketchbooks and viewpoints of where he painted landscapes such as the famous *Hay Wain*. Telephone: 01206 298260.

Pin Mill
The Butt & Oyster

MAP: OS EXPLORER 197 (GR 206380) **WALK 18** **DISTANCE:** 2 MILES

DIRECTIONS TO START: THE HAMLET OF PIN MILL LIES 6 MILES SOUTH-EAST OF
IPSWICH. TAKE THE B1456 SHOTLEY ROAD, TURN OFF AT CHELMONDISTON AND FOLLOW
THE ROAD SIGNS. **PARKING:** IF THERE IS NO ROOM IN THE PUB CAR PARK, TRY THE PAY
AND DISPLAY CAR PARK BESIDE THE APPROACH ROAD.

With a river frontage and cliff top woodland area, this short stroll is one of the most popular in Suffolk. Pin Mill is a hamlet of Chelmondiston and is also a well-known beauty spot that attracts walkers, yachtspeople and artists. The children's author Arthur Ransome, who wrote *Swallows and Amazons* and other books, once lived here. Further upstream you can see the stylish arches of the Orwell Bridge, opened in 1992. The Cliff Plantation, owned by the National Trust, runs alongside the Orwell estuary and is only accessible on foot. The great storm of 1987 wreaked havoc amongst the trees but a programme of replanting was carried out to provide the attractive woodland we see today. Towards the end of the walk as you approach the Butt and Oyster, you may have to retrace your steps a short distance due to the incoming tide.

The Butt & Oyster

Standing at the river's edge, tidal water quite literally laps the Butt & Oyster's walls. The bay windows offer a view of commercial shipping and pleasure craft making their way along the Orwell. The origins of this old bargemen's pub can be traced back to 1553 when it was first licensed. Local legends tell of its past association with revenue men pursuing smugglers engaged in the illegal landing of spirits and tobacco. Nowadays the atmospheric inn still retains a nautical flavour and has a comprehensive collection of paintings and model sailing ships. In the bar area, complete with high backed settles and benches on a tiled floor, metal trade signs hang beside fishing nets, old lamps and other objects based on a maritime theme. The main eating speciality here is fish, some of it caught and delivered from Lowestoft. In the restaurant you can choose from the likes of cod, plaice, mackerel, salmon and trout, with alternative dishes such as steaks, vegetable curry and steak and ale pie. Among the bar snacks there are sandwiches and baguettes filled with a variety of fish and salad fillings. The cask ales and draught beers available include Flowers, Adnams and Guinness. Well-behaved children are welcome but not in the bar area. During the warmer weather meals can be taken on tables positioned outside. The pub is open seven days a week and food is available daily. Telephone: 01473 780764.

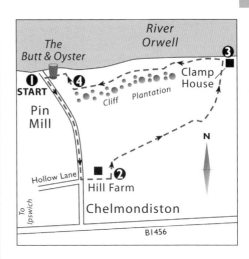

The Walk

① Come out of the car park and turn left onto the access road. You may well see the odd Thames sailing barge moored nearby on the river. Carry on along the steadily rising road, ignoring all turnings going left and right. Pass the pay and display car park and continue ahead to eventually reach Hollow Lane on the right. Turn left (signpost not apparent) almost opposite to join a bridleway.

② Keep veering left and shortly pass Hill Farm buildings. During spells of inclement weather conditions, you may have to dodge large puddles that form on the sandy path. Continue ahead and go past the entrance to the National Trust's Cliff Plantation. The path now starts to run downhill and provides some tantalising views of the Orwell in front. Go past a couple of small reservoirs on the right before passing through a kissing gate. Follow the woodland edge to arrive at Clamp House.

③ An uninterrupted view of the river at this vantage point provides a great photo

The River Orwell, Pin Hill

opportunity. To continue, turn left and go past a tiled barn to enter Cliff Plantation. Keep following a well-defined undulating path through the woodland. Occasional breaks in the hedgeline on the right provide scenic views across the river, including that of Orwell Park School, with its distinctive green dome. Notices indicate that the woodland is part of open access land which can be explored and enjoyed.

④ At the bottom of a steepish descent, turn right by a three-fingered post and follow a river edge path. Stay on the path and shortly pass some houseboats. If the tide is in as you approach the pub, retrace your steps back to a small wooden bridge. Climb up a line of steps cut into the bank

> ### PLACES OF INTEREST NEARBY
> The former village of Alton disappeared when the area was flooded to create a 2,000 million gallon water reservoir. Nowadays **Alton Water** – south-west of Chelmondiston and reached from the B1080 – is a popular place for fishing, sailing and bird watching. The site has a visitor centre and bikes can be hired to explore designated paths around the reservoir and the local countryside. Telephone: 01473 589105.

and turn right at the top. Pass through a kissing gate beside a paddock fence. Continue along the path and later bear right to go down some concrete steps. Turn right at the bottom and your point of return is just ahead by the river.

Witnesham
The Barley Mow

DIRECTIONS TO START: THE VILLAGE OF WITNESHAM LIES ABOUT 5 MILES NORTH
OF IPSWICH, WITH THE B1077 ROAD PASSING RIGHT BESIDE THE BARLEY MOW.
PARKING: PARK TO THE SIDE OF THE PUB.

From the main road there appears to be two quite separate communities either side of the Fynn valley. This stroll concentrates on the more interesting western side. Despite its closeness to the urban sprawl of Ipswich, the village still retains its own local identity and character. The well-known cartoonist Carl Giles was a resident of Witnesham before he died in 1995. His name and craft is perpetuated on the village sign, which features a row of typical Giles-style pigs behind a barred gate. As you pass through St Mary's churchyard, take a glance above the south door on the church tower. Here you will see a clock and a sundial, each thought to have been added during the 17th century. But why both? Along the way, the route progresses along the bottom of sloping fields and pasture and later crosses the small River Fynn. A major highlight is a long stretch of green lane, created perhaps to mark the parish and hundred boundary.

The Barley Mow

This was a dwelling house long before it became an inn. Around 1760 there is evidence of the property being described as 'now known by the name or sign of the Barley Mow'. Mow is an old term for a stack – hence 'Barley Mow'. Locally grown barley is a principle ingredient of beer. Hanging on a wall is a list of names of the pub's occupants since 1844. Also adorning the wall are some framed Giles cartoons. The bar and some cosy alcoves are in an area of exposed and low ceilings. During the winter, a warm, wood-burning stove greets you in the friendly locals' bar, where several real ales are offered. Chalked up on a blackboard is a wide range of pub food, which can be eaten in a separate dining area. The emphasis here is on home-made dishes such as curries and steak and kidney pudding. Traditional fish and chips is another firm favourite. For something lighter, sandwiches are available with a variety of fillings. There is also a good selection of desserts. Children are welcome and dogs are allowed in the bar area. Outside there is a pleasant beer garden. The pub is open Monday to Friday from 4.30 pm until closing time. Saturday and Sunday from 12 noon until closing time. Telephone: 01473 785395.

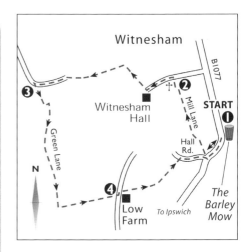

The Walk

① Cross the road in front and turn left onto the footway. Head down towards The Street and turn right at the war memorial. Enter Hall Road and quickly turn right to join Mill Lane. Follow the rising track to the point where it bears right. Go straight ahead into the next field and continue by a field edge path. Exit the field and pass through a kissing gate. Skirt a property on the left and pass in front of Manor Farm. Pass through a gate and cross a wooden bridge.

② Keep forward and take a permissive path that edges the village hall car park to reach the road in front. Turn left there and later pass a ford to arrive at Witnesham Hall. Bear right and continue along a stony path. Turn left at the boundary and carry on with a hedge on the left. Shortly the narrow path becomes surfaced and later widens beside a substantial house set back on the right. Stay on the road for another 300 yards to almost reach the point where

PLACES OF INTEREST NEARBY

Ipswich Museum, founded in 1847, contains one of the best collections of stuffed British birds in the country. Archaeological displays include specimens of minerals, fossils and rocks. The centrepiece is a natural history gallery that, amongst other things, features a giraffe, rhinoceros and woolly mammoth. Telephone: 01473 433550.

The ford of Witnesham

it bends sharp right. Turn left here beside a bridleway signpost.

③ With a plantation of trees on the left, head towards an entrance with a hedgerow either side. This is the start of a lengthy green lane. Stay on it for some distance before losing and later regaining the left hedge. Carry on for about another 600 yards and turn left through a hedge gap. Quickly turn right and left to follow a path, which acts as a field break. At the boundary go over a stile and head through pasture to reach Low Farm in front.

④ Turn left there onto a narrow lane and in 30 yards turn right into a field. Maintain direction across the field and look for a gap in the hedge on the other side. Turn right and follow the descending field edge path to the bottom boundary. Veer right a few paces into the adjoining field, go left over a stile and down a bank. Cross some pasture and aim towards the houses in front. Cross a small concrete bridge, go up a narrow path and turn right at the top to join Hall Road. Turn left at the other end and return to the Barley Mow.

Debenham
The Woolpack

MAP: OS EXPLORER 211 (GR 176631) **WALK 20** **DISTANCE:** 3 MILES

DIRECTIONS TO START: TAKE THE B1077 IPSWICH TO EYE ROAD, WHICH LEADS TO
CROSS GREEN CAR PARK ON THE RIGHT IN HIGH STREET, DEBENHAM.
PARKING: PARK AT CROSS GREEN CAR PARK IN THE HIGH STREET.

Debenham lies in the heart of the Suffolk countryside near the source of the River Deben, from where it gets its name. The picture postcard village was at one time a thriving wool centre as evidenced by the village sign and a wealth of merchants' timber-framed houses dating from the 14th century. Many of the old established businesses lining the main street have been supplying goods and services to successive generations. During recent years a number of antique shops have sprung up, drawing customers in from a wide area. The stroll sets off along the High Street and passes the interesting church of St Mary. After a climb up Gracechurch Street, you are rewarded with fine views of the village and surrounding countryside. The stroll later goes down and up the sides of a valley, before a leisurely return is made to the Woolpack.

The Woolpack

A warm welcome and a friendly atmosphere await you at this small pub nestling in Debenham's High Street. At one time there were some dozen pubs in Debenham but currently the Woolpack is the only one left. The village grew relatively wealthy from the medieval wool trade (sheep are depicted on the village sign) and that's possibly from where the pub originally got its name. From a menu chalked up on a board, there's a large choice of pub grub, including steaks, cod and chips, scampi and lasagne. The pub also does daily specials and a snack menu. Drinks include Greene King IPA, guest ales and cider obtained from a local brewery. Meals are served from 12 noon to 2 pm and 6.30 pm to 9 pm Tuesday to Saturday. Sunday lunch is also served. Telephone: 01728 860516.

The Walk

① Leave the car park, cross the road and turn right into High Street. Pass the Foresters Hall and the Woolpack pub opposite. Make a short detour if you wish to peep inside St Mary's church on the other side of the road. Carry on to reach the junction with Gracechurch Street, where the quaint market cross stands. It was reputedly built in the 17th century on a former Anglo Saxon site.

② Turn left and gradually proceed up to the top of Gracechurch Street from where some fine views of the Deben valley may be seen. Maintain direction to finally arrive at the high school and leisure centre. Carry on for a further 150 yards to reach a lamp post.

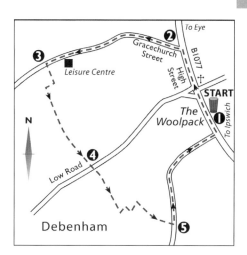

③ Turn left here and take a narrow path that runs between wire fences to emerge onto a playing field. Veer right and left beside the perimeter of the field. Pass under some overhead cables and go through an entrance into a cultivated field. Continue down a grassy path to reach the bottom of a shallow valley. Proceed over a concrete bridge with metal railings and turn left into Low Road.

④ After about 25 yards, turn right and enter a field to join a rising field edge path. The zig-zagging path eventually brings you to a two-finger signpost. Cross a bridge through a hedge gap and then take a cross-field path, aiming towards a bungalow situated at the far side of the field.

PLACES OF INTEREST NEARBY

Take a look round the nearby **Carter's teapot factory** and you can see how collectable teapots are made. From the viewing area, you can watch the highly skilled staff take the teapots from their moulds, carefully put them together and paint them. Telephone: 01728 860475.

Corner of Gracechurch Street, Debenham

(5) Turn left onto the road and walk back towards Debenham village. After 150 yards turn right into a field entrance, swing left and continue along a broad field margin introduced by the Countryside Stewardship Scheme. Carry on to eventually reach the bottom boundary and turn left to join the Ipswich road. Follow the footway past Kenton Road and your point of departure is further ahead on the right.

Stradbroke
The Queen's Head

MAP: OS EXPLORER 230 (GR 230740)   **WALK 21**   DISTANCE: 3½ MILES

DIRECTIONS TO START: LEAVE THE A140 NORWICH-IPSWICH ROAD AT YAXLEY AND FOLLOW THE B1117 THROUGH EYE TO STRADBROKE. THE VILLAGE CAN ALSO BE APPROACHED FROM FRAMLINGHAM AND DISS BY THE B1118. **PARKING:** PARK IN THE CAR PARK AT THE REAR OF THE PUB.

From whatever direction you enter Stradbroke, the road passes between swathes of cultivated fields with isolated farm buildings. Positioned either side of a busy crossroads, this large village stands exposed amongst the rural heartlands of the Suffolk-Norfolk border. Stradbroke is an old settlement with an Anglo Saxon name that means a place where a Roman road (strad) crosses a brook. It is a thriving community with several shops, pubs, a high school and sports facilities, including an indoor swimming pool. Thatched cottages, timber-framed houses and small housing estates blend together side by side. Standing in the village centre is the 15th century church of All Saints, built with wealth from the medieval wool trade. It's said that twelve parishes can be seen from the top of the tower. Stradbroke has a good network of paths, some of which are used on this stroll to explore the village character and flavour.

The Queen's Head

An odd fact about Queen Street, where the pub stands, is that it was named after the pub itself. The Grade II listed building with its timber-framed interior and brick façade, dates back to the 17th century, although there have been many alterations since. The hostelry, situated near the centre of the village, welcomes walkers and serves good old fashioned pub grub. For instance, from an ever changing menu, choices include the likes of home-made lasagne, ham, egg and chips, sausage and mash, steak and ale pie and cod and chips. A traditional roast is served on Sundays. Bar snacks include baguettes, sandwiches and ploughman's. Food can be eaten in the bar or in a separate dining area. For drinks, some of which are served by hand pumps, there's Adnam's bitter plus a choice of IPA, Woodeforde's Wherry and other guest beers. During the better weather there's a beer garden in which to relax. The pub is open all day from 12 noon onwards. It's advisable to book in advance, especially at weekends and bank holidays. Telephone: 01379 384384.

The Walk

① Leave the pub, turn right and head towards the road junction in front. Turn right and then left to join Wilby Road. Walk past the fire station on the right and the entrance to Stradbroke High School a little further on. Just after passing the last house on the left, bear left to join a narrow path, which runs beside a field edge. Continue, with a hedge on the left, until you reach Neaves Lane.

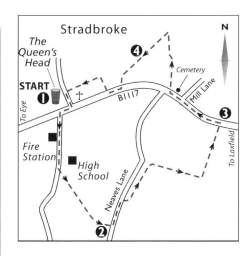

② Turn left. In about 300 yards, turn right over a culvert to enter a field. Turn left and follow a field edge path and later go over a sleeper bridge. Cross a cultivated field and go over a wooden bridge on the other side. Turn right, stay in the field and follow the headland round to meet the B1117.

③ Turn left here and follow the road past Mill Lane. Just after passing the entrance to the village cemetery, turn right. Carry on along a path, which shortly becomes concreted and later develops into a grassy way. Before reaching a footpath signpost in front, turn sharp left, with Stradbroke church tower positioned just to the left. Take a well-defined path over a cultivated field, passing a lone oak tree in the process. Turn left at the boundary.

④ Stay on the path as it gently descends Drapers Hill. At the bottom, turn left and right to rejoin the B1117 once again. In 50 yards, turn right into Shenton Hill and shortly left into Willow Close. Bear left at the far end and go past the old village pond,

The mural on the fire station wall

which may be partially obscured by vegetation. Continue ahead, pass between a metal barrier and turn left when you reach Queen Street. Cross the road to find the pub almost opposite.

PLACES OF INTEREST NEARBY

Further east along the B1117, **Laxfield Guildhall** is an attractive 15th-century timber-framed structure with brick nogging. A museum, located on the first floor of this Grade II listed building, contains a display on rural, domestic and working life during previous centuries. Other collections feature items on local archaeology and natural history. Telephone: 01986 798026 or 798460.

Charsfield
The Three Horseshoes

MAP: OS EXPLORER 212 (GR 254564) | **WALK 22** | **DISTANCE:** 3½ MILES

DIRECTIONS TO START: LEAVE THE A140 AT BEACON HILL INTERCHANGE AND TAKE THE B1078 THROUGH CODDENHAM AND THENCE TO CHARSFIELD. GO LEFT ON A MINOR ROAD SIGNPOSTED TO FRAMLINGHAM AND HEAD FOR 'THE STREET'.
PARKING: THERE IS A LARGE PARKING AREA BESIDE THE PUB.

The scattered village of Charsfield lies mainly at the bottom of a valley in a rural landscape. At one time most of the local population was engaged in some way or another in agriculture. In the late 19th century a large acreage of land was replanted with fruit orchards, replacing traditional cereal crops. On this stroll, undulating paths take you beside fields of currant bushes and apple trees, best seen perhaps during fruit blossom time in late April early May. Elsewhere, standing beside quiet country lanes, you'll find period cottages intermingling with farmhouses and packing sheds. Charsfield was the fictitious *Akenfield*, a classic book about village life written by Ronald Blythe and later made into a film using local people as actors. Nowadays, sadly, many of the professions and characters mentioned in the book have long since disappeared.

The Three Horseshoes

Expect a friendly greeting as you enter the Three Horseshoes, a pub originating from the mid 1800s and at the heart of the local community. Adorning the walls in the refurbished pub are photographs displaying village activities past and present. Elsewhere, old posters along with branded beer and spirit bottles – minus their contents – evoke pleasant memories of yesteryear. Meals may be taken in the bar area or in the restaurant. From an extensive menu you have the choice of dishes such as ham, egg and chips, plaice and chips, home-made shepherd's pie, liver and bacon and a traditional roast (Sunday lunch only). Lite bites, plus a selection of sandwiches and baguettes are also served. Tempting desserts include treacle pudding, chocolate puddle pudding and fruit crumble. A senior citizens' menu is also available. Drinks include Victorian bitter, brewed locally, plus a guest ale. Food is served daily from 12 noon to 2 pm and 7 pm to 9 pm except Thursday when the pub is closed all day. Booking is advisable for the restaurant. Telephone: 01473 737330.

The Walk

① Turn left out of the car park, carry on along the village street and eventually reach the Baptist chapel. Turn left to join Chapel Lane and continue on a steadily rising surface and afterwards descend again to reach a T-junction.

② Turn right here, keep straight ahead for about 100 yards and then turn left into Magpie Street. Stay on the road for about

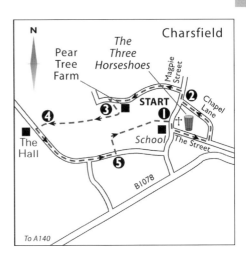

another 800 yards to arrive at Pear Tree Farm. Just past the farm look for a fingerpost beside the road. Here, go left through a gap in the hedge to enter a cultivated field.

③ Continue on a broad field margin, with a hedge on the left. Turn right at the boundary, still with a hedge on the left. The path heads slightly downhill and is later replaced by a surfaced access track.

④ Continue along the track, which finally leads to The Hall, a short distance away in front. However, before reaching the house, where the track bears left, turn left over a stile and cross a short stretch of pasture. Veer right to go over a ditch and then a footbridge. Pass through a wooden gate and turn left onto the road, following it to a junction and keeping straight on.

⑤ Just before reaching the next bungalow on the left, turn left onto a muddy farm track. At the far end turn right onto another track, which leads in the direction of the church seen in the distance ahead.

The Baptist church, Charsfield

After passing the primary school turn right onto the road and soon turn left to enter The Street once again. The pub is just ahead on the left.

PLACES OF INTEREST NEARBY

Easton Farm Park, set in 35 acres of beautiful rural Suffolk at Easton to the north-east of Charsfield, offers an opportunity for the whole family to relax and learn about the countryside and its way of living at first hand. Exhibits include a Victorian dairy and vintage working machinery. Farmers' markets are held here on the last Saturday of every month. Telephone: 01728 746475.

Framlingham
The Station Hotel

MAP: OS EXPLORER 212 (GR 284630)   **WALK 23**   **DISTANCE:** 2½ MILES

DIRECTIONS TO START: TURN OFF THE A1120 STOWMARKET-YOXFORD ROAD AT SAXTEAD GREEN. TAKE THE B1119 INTO FRAMLINGHAM AND TURN RIGHT AT THE FIRST JUNCTION. AT THE NEXT JUNCTION CARRY STRAIGHT ON DOWN STATION ROAD (B1116) TO FIND THE STATION HOTEL ON THE RIGHT.
PARKING: IN THE YARD BESIDE THE PUB.

The historic town of Framlingham is well known for its castle and to a lesser extent for its college buildings. Both feature on this easy stroll, which the whole family can enjoy. The castle especially can be viewed to advantage from a number of angles as you make your way round. When seen from afar, the prevailing light and shade give the thirteen towers and curtain wall a very different perspective to that of the normal close-up view. Don't forget to take a camera with you. Some stunning shots can be obtained of the castle mere, with the castle itself making an impressive backdrop. The Suffolk Wildlife Trust notice board invites you to enter the Mere nature reserve, where cattle can often be found grazing on the marshes.

The Station Hotel

The Station Hotel, as the name suggests, is a former railway station buffet (c1859). It occupies part of the buildings left redundant when the Framlingham to Saxmundham branch line finally closed in 1963. Inside the spacious bar room, a fine set of Edwardian hand pumps on the bar, paintings and photos of trains, a wooden floor, scrubbed tables and chairs all add character and are atmospheric reminders of times past. From an inviting menu chalked up on the board that caters for all tastes, light lunch choices include dishes such as sausage and mash, steak and ale pudding, plus favourites like ploughman's, open sandwiches and bacon baps. Meat and fish steaks and other substantial meals are also available, together with a choice of home-made desserts. Popular real ales from a local micro brewery are on offer, along with ever-changing guest beers. Children and dogs are welcome. Currrent opening times are 12 noon to 2.30 pm and 5 pm to 11 pm. Telephone: 01728 723455.

The Walk

① Leave the pub and walk towards the town centre. In a few paces turn right and take the narrow surfaced path over a green area. Cross over a bridge and turn left into Fairfield Road. Continue along the footway and cross the road junction ahead. Pass some public toilets and afterwards turn right to join Castle Street.

② Continue towards Framlingham Castle that gradually comes into view. Just short of the castle entrance turn right through a gate to enter Castle Meadows. With the castle walls and earthworks on the left,

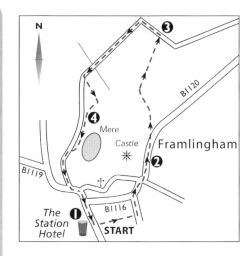

head straight acorss the grass. Locate a hedge gap and follow the path to a smaller green area. Walk beside the hedge opposite and shortly turn right as directed by a marker post to reach the Badingham road.

③ Turn left and continue along a footway. After about 200 yards turn left again down some concrete steps in the bank. Carry on beside a field edge with a hedge on the right. Go over a footbridge into the adjoining field and shortly enter the next one. Bear right past a three-way marker

PLACES OF INTEREST NEARBY

Framlingham Castle dates back to the 12th century, and can be accessed via Church Street. Telephone: 01728 724189. **Saxtead Green Post Mill** standing beside the A1120, is one of the best preserved post mills in the country. The present mill, dating from about 1706, has been refurbished and is in excellent working order. You can climb up the wooden stairs, watch the mechanism and enjoy an audio tour that describes the milling process. Telephone: 01728 685789.

Framlingham Castle

post to eventually meet a road where you turn left. Continue to the bottom of the hill and turn left.

④ Continue ahead on the surfaced road and later ignore a path going left. Immediately after crossing a road bridge over the infant River Ore, leave the road and turn left to skirt a large shed on the right. Enter the playing fields of Framlingham College and stay on the left edge. Make your way round the field's perimeter to arrive at the far right corner. You have a choice of paths here. Go up some concrete steps if you wish and turn left at the top onto a road that will take you back to your start point. Otherwise, go through a kissing gate to enter the Framlingham Mere Nature Reserve belonging to the Suffolk Wildlife Trust.

⑤ Follow the path that runs parallel to the road and exit the reserve by the last kissing gate. Turn left onto the road, pass the Elms car park and cross Bridge Street. Maintain direction to reach Station Road and follow the footway back to your starting point, another 200 yards ahead on the right.

Woodbridge
The Cherry Tree

MAP: OS EXPLORER 197 OR 212 (GR 268486)   **WALK 24**   **DISTANCE:** 2½ MILES

DIRECTIONS TO START: LEAVE THE A12 AT THE WOODBRIDGE TURN OFF AND CONTINUE TOWARDS THE TOWN CENTRE ON THE B1438. THE PUB IS ON THE RIGHT IN CUMBERLAND STREET, OPPOSITE NOTCUTTS GARDEN CENTRE. **PARKING:** THERE IS A LARGE CAR PARK TO THE REAR OF THE PUB.

The Cherry Tree pub is a convenient place from which to explore this picturesque part of Woodbridge, a small town with fine Tudor and Georgian buildings and steeped in history. Shortly after leaving the town area the Woodland Trust welcomes you to briefly enter and follow an undulating path through Porter's Wood, part of a delightful area marked on the map as Maidensgrave. A descending path takes you to Kyson Hill, a National Trust beauty spot from where spectacular views across the River Deben and beyond may be obtained. A path beside the Deben allows a closer look at the colourful array of sailing craft, moorings and boatyards to be found here. Further ahead lies the restored 18th-century tide mill, the only survivor of its kind in Britain and open to the public.

The Cherry Tree

Just as you are about to step into the Cherry Tree, you are greeted by Dante's famous dictum: 'All hope abandon, ye who enter here'. This and other quotations, mostly humorous, were stencilled on the ceiling and walls by a previous tenant. Once inside, you'll find a welcome smile from staff behind a U-shaped bar, which forms part of a spacious area where a low ceiling is supported by heavy wooden beams. Situated not far from the town centre, it's thought that the pub, which originated during the 17th century and is currently a listed building, is named after a large cherry tree that stood at the entrance to what is now Cherry Tree Road. Popular favourites from a comprehensive menu include traditional roasts, steak and mushroom pie, sweet and sour pork with rice and a range of steak and fish dishes. Sweet courses include banana splits, Bakewell tart, spotted dick and treacle pudding. For drinks there is a choice of Adnams cask ales, including Best Bitter and Broadside, plus a selection of other beers and lagers. The pub is open daily and it's advisable to book for meals at weekends. At the rear of the premises there is a large patio garden with a children's play area. The Cherry Tree is well known for its floral displays. Telephone: 01394 384627.

The Walk

① From the pub turn left and walk up the hill. Turn right into Warren Hill Road and continue on a steady climb along the footway, passing a cemetery on the right. When you reach the top of the hill, turn

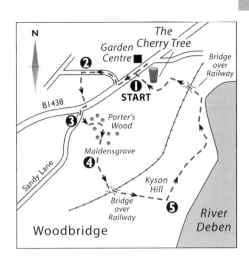

left onto a footpath opposite Portal Crescent.

② Continue on a narrow path, which runs between some rear gardens, until you reach a flight of steps. Go down the latter and cross the Ipswich road with care at the bottom. Turn right and after a short distance turn left to join the surfaced Sandy Lane.

③ Carry on along Sandy Lane and just before reaching a phone box, turn left to join some woodland owned by the Woodland Trust. Keep straight ahead on a well-defined path, passing a marker post, with a yellow badge, on the left. Stay on the path as it meanders through the woods.

④ In front of you is a lovely area known as Broomheath. Maintain direction through an avenue of trees and houses set well back from the road. Keep following the road and eventually cross a bridge over the railway. Soon you will see occasional views of the Deben through the trees as you approach the scenic area of Kyson Hill. Turn left at

Sailing on the River Deben, Woodbridge

the bottom of the hill to join a tarmac path.

⑤ Continue along the path with pasture on the left and the river on the right. If you wish to visit the Tide Mill carry straight on to the far end. Otherwise, just after passing a sailing clubhouse, look for a toilet block. Pass the latter and go over a rail crossing in front. At a road junction turn left to join Kingston Farm Road. After about 60 yards turn right into Cherry Tree Road. Your start point is just ahead on the right.

PLACES OF INTEREST NEARBY
The Suffolk Horse Museum is located in the town's Shire Hall. Here you will find displays relating to the Suffolk Punch, which is the oldest breed of working horse in Great Britain. Paintings and photographs on view help to illustrate the importance and rarity of this fine animal. Telephone: 01394 380643.

Sutton
The Plough

DIRECTIONS TO START: LEAVE THE A12 AT THE ROUNDABOUT JUST NORTH OF WOODBRIDGE AND TAKE THE A1152. GO THROUGH MELTON AND THEN FOLLOW THE B1083 ROAD SIGNS TO SUTTON VILLAGE. **PARKING:** THERE IS A LARGE CAR PARK BESIDE THE PUB.

The Suffolk Sandlings, which feature on this enjoyable stroll, are classified as lowland heath and confirmed as one of Britain's rarest habitats. At one time the Sandlings stretched continuously from the outskirts of Ipswich along the northern edge of the county to Lowestoft. The heaths are man-made habitats, created for sheep grazing during the medieval period. From the Plough pub the stroll takes you through a large expanse of Sutton Heath, a scene little changed over the years. As the Sandlings name suggests, you will find plenty of sand along the route. Locals claim there is more sand in the area than can be found on nearby Bawdsey Beach. Walking through a lonely landscape of bracken and heather, you might, if you are very lucky, encounter unusual bird species such as the woodlark and nightjar, and also catch a glimpse of a silver-studded butterfly.

The Plough

After a period of sporadic trading, the Plough has now re-opened. The pub stands in the sparsely populated village of Sutton beside the B1083 Melton–Bawdsey road. Once inside, you'll find a small bar area and a room containing a bar billiard table and dart board. An inviting menu features dishes such as cod and chips, ham, egg and chips, lasagne and scampi. On Thursdays there is a special meal offer for senior citizens. For drinks, the likes of Fosters, IPA and Carlsberg, plus guest ales, are on tap. There is a beer garden in which to relax, plus a children's play area next to an ample car park. Telephone: 01394 411785.

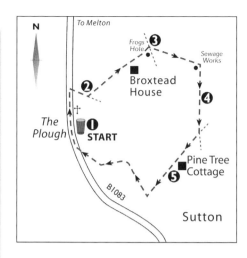

The Walk

① Turn right out of car park and set off beside the main road. You may have to walk on the bank in places to avoid any oncoming traffic. Pass the entrances to the parish church and Church Farm respectively before taking the next turning right to join a gravel access road. Carry on down the road and shortly turn left, ignoring a path leading to Broxtead House.

② Continue along a partially concreted path beside a long line of trees, which includes varieties such as oak and sweet chestnut. Shortly pass some farm out-buildings and ignore a sandy path going right. Keep going straight ahead, with a hedge on the left to reach a belt of pine trees.

③ Follow the path as it curves right, shortly walking parallel with a stretch of chain link fencing on the right. Follow the fence round and maintain direction through areas of bracken for about 500 yards to eventually reach and climb over a stile beside a long metal gate.

④ With an area of woodland on the left, carry straight on along a bridleway path. When you reach a crossroads of paths, turn right. Carry on ahead and later gently descend along a path with hedgerows either side.

⑤ Just after passing Pine Tree Cottage on the left, continue straight ahead, passing

PLACES OF INTEREST NEARBY

In 1939 a huge ship grave was unearthed at nearby **Sutton Hoo**, which is just off the B1083 south of Melton. An exhibition tells the story of how priceless treasures were discovered at the Anglo Saxon burial site, now acquired by the National Trust. There is a full re-creation of the ship burial and displays of original objects. Waymarked paths lead to the burial mounds. Telephone: 01394 389700.

Sutton Common

the odd house on the right. Hereabouts the amount of sand underfoot is particularly noticeable. Soon, however, you reach a surfaced access road, albeit dusted with sand. Swing right ahead to pass some farm buildings on the left. When the road curves left at the far end, carry straight on for about 50 yards. Turn left through a field entrance and continue along the field edge with a hedge on the left. Follow the field edge, which finally brings you back beside the pub.

Sibton
The White Horse

DIRECTIONS:TAKE THE A1120 STOWMARKET-YOXFORD ROAD. JUST EAST OF
THE POST OFFICE IN PEASENHALL, TURN LEFT AND FOLLOW THE ROAD TO SIBTON.
THE WHITE HORSE IS A MILE OR SO FURTHER ON. **PARKING:** THERE IS AMPLE PARKING
NEXT TO THE PUB.

Motorists using the A1120 often bypass Sibton in their haste to reach the coast – a further fifteen minutes or so away. However, it would be a shame not to break the journey once in a while and make the short detour to Sibton, a small village full of history and character. In Old English the place name equates to 'Sibba's Farmstead'. Over the centuries the area has retained its historic farmhouses; a couple of the more substantial ones, still used as working farms, can be seen as you make your way round. Much of this easy stroll takes you amongst sloping fields and quiet paths set in a shallow valley. In places you have a tributary of the River Yox, or maybe the Yox itself, for company. The river is not all that deep or wide – in parts more like a water channel perhaps.

The White Horse

Standing prominently in its position near a road junction, the White Horse is extremely popular with locals and visitors alike. Part of the building apparently survives from the 1300s, although most of the pub was burnt down in 1665 and rebuilt a year later. Bricks taken from a nearby Roman road were incorporated in the construction of the cellar. Some of the timber beams supporting the low ceilings are thought to have been obtained from wrecked ships at Dunwich. The centrepiece of the bar lounge is a large brick fireplace displaying some horsey memorabilia, including horse brasses and harness. Elsewhere there is an assortment of plates and lamps. Furniture includes wooden tables and some high-backed chairs and benches. The menu is varied and wholesome. Typical dishes on the menu include beer-battered cod, gammon steak and home minced venison burger. The pub also does a selection of sandwiches on wholemeal or granary bread, accompanied by a bowl of chips if desired. Drinks include Adnam's Bitter and Broadside, plus weekly-changed guest ales. Well-behaved children and dogs are welcome. Booking is advised for meals, especially at weekends. Telephone: 01728 660337.

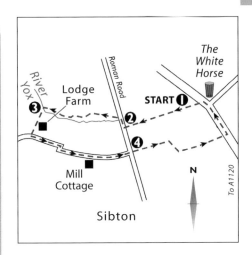

The Walk

① From the pub turn right and in about 50 yards turn left by a footpath sign. Cross a bridge and continue on the other side beside the infant River Yox on the left and a paddock fence on the right. Keep forward and later cross a footbridge to swing left and right with a hedge on the right.

Continue ahead along the left edge of some pasture at the bottom of a sloping field.

② Maintain direction and aim towards a minor road in front. Turn right here and in about 100 yards turn left to carry on along a field edge path with a hedge on the left. Just after passing a scrap metal area, turn left, go forward and afterwards turn right. Continue walking beside the river channel on a broad grassy path. Ignore a path going left over a culvert to Vale Farm and continue straight on.

③ Take a left turn over a concrete slabbed bridge and make your way up a steadily rising farm track. Go past Lodge Farm and

PLACES OF INTEREST NEARBY

The bird reserve at **Minsmere** – across the A12 to the east of Sibton – is the jewel in the RSPB's crown. A great variety of birds, especially in the breeding season, can be seen in a large area of heath, woods, reedbeds and lagoon. There is an attractive visitor centre, waymarked trails and bird hides. Telephone: 01728 648281.

Along the route near Sibton

turn left when you finally meet the road ahead. Stay on the road as it ambles its way through part of Sibton village. As you pass Mill Cottage, look right to see what appears to be part of the old mill buildings. Soon the road descends towards a T-junction. Cross straight over and go up some steps in the bank opposite.

④ Continue along a field edge path with a hedge on the right. Enter the next field, turn right and follow the path as it soon curves left. After passing a small pond, your way ahead goes down a slight dip to meet a narrow sunken path. Stay on the latter until you reach the road. Turn left and walk along the footway back to the White Horse.

Mill Common, Westhall
The Racehorse

MAP: OS EXPLORER 231 (GR 409818)   **WALK 27**   **DISTANCE:** 4 MILES

DIRECTIONS TO START: LEAVE THE A12 NORTH OF BLYTHBURGH AND TAKE THE A145 BLYTHBURGH-BECCLES ROAD. TURN LEFT AT BRAMTON CHURCH AND FOLLOW THE ROAD SIGNS TO WESTHALL VILLAGE CENTRE. MILL COMMON AND THE PUB ARE REACHED JUST AFTER ENTERING THE BUILT-UP AREA. **PARKING:** PARK IN FRONT OF THE RACEHORSE OR AT THE VILLAGE HALL NEXT DOOR.

If you like exploring historic churches, then this is the walk for you. St Andrew's, Westhall stands isolated from the present village although it was at one time surrounded by farm cottages and a manor house. It's said that most of the modern village – to the west around Mill Common – was established when the East Suffolk Railway, built in the mid 1800s, finally reached nearby Brampton. After a walk through the unspoilt countryside that links the two villages, you eventually reach the church. When it was enlarged in the 14th century, instead of demolishing and replacing the 12th-century building they built a grand new nave on the side of it. Inside, treasures include a 16th-century font, a magnificent painted rood screen and a must-see Norman doorway hidden behind a closed curtain.

The Racehorse

How many pubs across the county are known by the name of the Racehorse? I certainly can't recall any locally. Was it originally named after a famous racehorse, I wondered, or maybe it was linked with a local horse of some distinction? Despite quizzing the locals, I left the pub none the wiser. Mind you, there are horsey connections inside. Hanging on the walls are pictures and paintings of horses as well as a harness in the bar lounge. The Racehorse – which is quite small – is a traditional village pub. Entrances from the bar lead to a bar lounge and a compact public bar the other side, which includes an area set aside for playing darts. Standing on a shelf are a number of sports trophies belonging to the local football club that plays across the way. Served in the small restaurant is a range of tasty dishes, including battered cod, lasagne, steak, chicken, mustard and herb pork and scampi. Details of specials and desserts are marked on a board. For drinks there is a selection of Adnams and other real ales. It's a good idea to book food in advance – with a small kitchen the licensee can only cope with a limited amount of customers at one time. The pub is open seven days a week but food is not available on Tuesdays. Well-behaved children and dogs are welcome. Telephone: 01502 575706.

The Walk

① Turn left onto the main road and in 100 yards or so reach some bungalows on the right. Turn right by a bus shelter (hidden), carry on to a kissing gate and

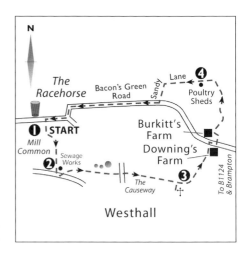

then take a field edge path. Shortly bear left and follow a cross-field path, which soon runs beside a hedge and ditch. Follow the path to a sewage plant and walk between a chain link fence and a hedge to emerge onto the road.

② Turn left here and continue along the road. In about 250 yards turn left again and initially walk beside a bank with a large pond on the right. Carry on by a field edge path with a stream running on the right. Skirt an area of woodland ahead and later go straight over the Causeway. This is a lonely stretch with the silence occasionally

PLACES OF INTEREST NEARBY

Halesworth & District Museum is located in the town's railway station, reached along the B1124 to the south of Westhall. Attractions include local history, railway and rural life exhibitions. The station's unique movable platforms are adjacent to the museum. There are also other displays relating to geology and archaeology, including finds from recent excavations. Telephone: 01986 875351.

In the village of Westhall

broken by birdsong or the rippling stream. Maintain direction through successive fields to finally arrive beside a path leading to Westhall church.

③ After visiting the church, return to this point and follow the path where it gradually curves left and steadily rises through a green corridor to finally reach Downing's Farm in front on the right. Turn right onto the road and in a further 150 yards go left to skirt Burkitt's farmyard. Cross a sleeper bridge at the boundary, swing left through a small thicket and afterwards turn right onto a farm track.

Continue ahead for about 600 yards and fork left to reach a three-finger signpost ahead where you turn left.

④ Go past some poultry sheds on the left and continue ahead on a bridleway. Soon you will join a lovely green lane marked on the map as Sandy Lane. Keep forward and stay on the lane, where mature hedgerows remain intact. Eventually, the lane bears left and afterwards meets the junction with Bacon's Green Road. Turn right here and follow the quiet road for the next mile or so back to your start point.

Snape
The Plough and Sail

MAP: OS EXPLORER 212 (GR 392575)	WALK 28	DISTANCE: 3 MILES

DIRECTIONS TO START: SNAPE MALTINGS IS SITUATED BESIDE THE B1069 ROAD, WHICH RUNS SOUTH FROM THE A1094 TO THE WEST OF ALDEBURGH.
PARKING: PARK IN FRONT OF THE PUB OR IN THE MALTINGS CAR PARK.

This interesting stroll starts from Snape Maltings, where Suffolk barley was once malted and sent to distant markets by boat on the adjacent Alde river. Original buildings, constructed in 1854 by a local Victorian businessman named Newson Garrett, have been converted into art and craft shops and antique rooms. A 19th-century granary building was transformed into the well-known Snape Maltings Concert Hall, which draws singers and musicians from all over the world. Sited beside the river path is a set of sculptures by Barbara Hepworth. Elsewhere on this absorbing walk you'll find delightful stretches of wood and heathland. From the Iken Cliff picnic site there is a distant sighting of Iken church standing on a promontory. There are also spectacular views across the upper reaches of the Alde. The mudflats and salt marshes are internationally important feeding grounds and migration sites for wading birds and wildfowl.

The Plough and Sail

Still an integral part of the Maltings complex, this popular pub has been extensively renovated and extended over recent years. As you pass through the main entrance, the bar is straight in front of you. Off to the left are three small rooms furnished with pine tables and chairs, which provide a cosy atmosphere. You can also relax on a high back settle with a log fire in front on cold days. Positioned on a wall is a large board that lists dates of historic occasions relating to the Snape Bridge area. A light and airy restaurant has been added to the original pub. Part of the stylish furniture includes some high-backed cane chairs. Photographs of tradesmen who built the original maltings hang on a wall and another wall contains a frieze that summarises the malting process. The 75 seater restaurant offers a light lunch menu with choices such as ploughman's, home-made soup and toasted paninis. Alternatively, you may opt for something more substantial like steaks and roasts from the à la carte menu. Drinks include a choice of beer and cask ales as well as wine, tea and coffee. The pub is open seven days a week and food is available daily. Telephone: 01728 688413.

The Walk

① Leave the pub and turn left to pass the Maltings complex. Bear right when you reach a triangular stretch of grass just ahead. After about 300 yards, fork right and take the road signposted to Blaxhall. Stay on the road for another 800 yards to reach a narrow road going right. Turn left opposite to enter a woodland area through a gap in the hedge.

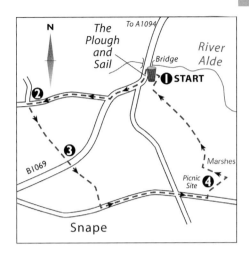

② Bear right by a marker post (marked with a black outline of a nightjar) to join the Suffolk Sandlings path. Carry on along the rising path on light soils. The walk shortly passes through part of Blaxhall Heath. When you finally reach the B1069 road ahead, cross straight over, with care.

③ Ignore all tracks going left and right and stay on the path as it runs ahead through bracken and belts of pine trees. Turn left when you reach a minor road. On either side of the road are areas of woodland, which provide a pleasant interlude. When you reach some crossroads, carry on straight ahead. Soon the tidal River Alde will appear, with the high ground providing a lovely vista across the water and marshes. After about 250 yards, turn left onto a track, which brings you to the Iken Cliff picnic site.

④ Pass the wooden statue of St Botolph and aim for the bottom left-hand corner of the sloping site to join a field edge path. Stay on the path as it twists and turns through the tall reedbeds. To ease walking

The Concert Hall and sculptures

over boggy stretches a lengthy section of boardwalk has been laid. Look out for birds such as pipits, reed warblers and the occasional kingfisher. You may see loads of gulls on the river, often put to flight by an overhead bird of prey. Cross a wooden bridge over a water channel and turn right at a T-junction of paths. Follow the path and pass Snape Concert Hall before finally entering the Maltings car park.

PLACES OF INTEREST NEARBY

The **Long Shop Museum** at Leiston, across the A1094 to the north-east of Snape, is the home of the Garrett collection – 200 years of local, social and industrial history. It's an award-winning museum housed on the original Garrett works site. The Grade II listed 1852 long shop, built by Richard Garrett, was one of Great Britain's first production lines for steam engines. Telephone: 01728 832189.

Orford
The Jolly Sailor

DIRECTIONS TO START: TURN OFF THE A12 AT THE ROUNDABOUT JUST NORTH OF WOODBRIDGE TO JOIN THE A1152 AND THEN TAKE THE B1084 TO ORFORD.
PARKING: AT THE PUB, OR IN THE PUBLIC PAY AND DISPLAY CAR PARK OPPOSITE.

Orford was an important town during the Middle Ages, and a short detour from the route of this stroll allows you to visit Orford Castle, built by Henry ll between 1163 and 1175. It is noteworthy for the unique design of its polygonal keep and for being one of the earliest castles to use mural or flanking towers along the curtain wall. Writing in 1722, however, Daniel Defoe declared that 'the town is now decayed. The sea daily throws up more land so it is a seaport no longer.' On this delightful circuit you can look across the river towards Orfordness, a 10 mile long shingle spit that constantly reacts to the forces of nature. Well-known landmarks on the Ness are the so-called pagoda buildings, where atomic bombs were tested to assess their resilience to accident.

The Jolly Sailor

Step down inside the Jolly Sailor pub and you immediately encounter a nautical atmosphere. On the walls, alongside a wood-burning fire set in a large brick fireplace, there is a selection of naval memorabilia, which includes photographs, model ships and charts. The original pub dates back to the 1700s and the building has welcomed seafarers and visitors ever since. Located only a few minutes walk from the quay, it once had the reputation of being an old smugglers' inn. It's thought that the wooden beams come from timbers of ships wrecked on nearby Orfordness. Somewhat unusually, the food and drink comes from small counters and hatches in an old-fashioned central cubicle. The real ales are the various Adnams brews. The food speciality here is delicious fried fish (and chips) such as cod, skate and rock eel. The pub has won numerous awards for the quality of its fish, freshly caught by local fishermen. Other dishes on offer include home-made lasagne, ham, egg and chips, pheasant in season and daily roasts. Desserts range from a selection of puddings and pies with custard and ice cream to fruit gateau. The Jolly Sailor is open all week but no meals are served in the restaurant on Monday evenings. Children under 14 are not permitted in the bar area. Dogs are allowed on a lead. Meals may be eaten outside at tables situated in the rear garden. B&B is available. Telephone: 01394 450243.

The Walk

① Leave the pub and turn right to walk towards Orford Quay. Turn right by a tile

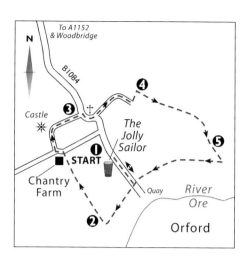

and wood shelter and continue along the river foreshore. Go through a kissing gate and up some steps the other side. Turn left and continue along the river wall. Where the latter bends left, come off the bank, go down a slope and head towards a wooden bridge in front.

② Cross the bridge and follow a broad grassy path to eventually reach Chantry Farm. Pass between some farm buildings and bear right at a road junction. Head towards the castle in front and make a short detour if you wish to explore the castle keep. Otherwise, stay on the slightly rising road and cross the town square.

PLACES OF INTEREST NEARBY

Take a brief ferryboat ride from the quay and cross to **Orfordness**. From 1913 to 1985 the Ness was a secret military establishment. Now that it has been acquired by the National Trust, you can walk along marked trails and discover something of the Ness's fascinating history, including bombs, bunkers and birds. Telephone: 01394 450057.

Orford Castle

③ Go straight ahead where the road curves right and go past St Bartholomew's church. Just after passing house no 26, turn right to join a short stretch of lane. Turn left at the bottom and, just beyond High House, turn right by a public footpath sign.

④ Go through a gate to follow a grassy path with a hedge initially on the right. Maintain direction and head towards Orford Lighthouse sited on the distant Ness. When you reach a field corner, turn right over a ditch and take a path which heads in the direction of the bank opposite.

⑤ Cross a watercourse over a stile and go up some wooden steps. Turn right at the top to join the river wall. Make your way along what is now the Suffolk Coast and Heaths path and pass Orford Sailing Club House. Leave the path by some wooden steps and swing back onto the quay. Keep veering right and follow the road previously walked, back to your departure point.

Thorpeness
The Dolphin

DIRECTIONS TO START: FROM BENHALL LEAVE THE A12 AND TAKE THE A1094 TO ALDEBURGH. JUST BEFORE REACHING THE SEA FRONT IN ALDEBURGH, TURN LEFT AT A T-JUNCTION AND FOLLOW A MINOR ROAD TO THORPENESS. **PARKING:** PARKING IS AVAILABLE IN THE PUB YARD.

Around 1910 the small village of Thorpeness was transformed into a model seaside resort by members of the Ogilvie family. A 65 acre lake was created where rowing boats could be (and still are) hired to explore the small artificial islands and associated wildlife. Later a golf course was added along with mock Tudor houses. Although disguised as a house and holiday home, the structure known as the House In The Clouds is in fact a water tower. The adjacent windmill was moved from nearby Aldringham in 1922 to pump water into the tower. The mill's lower interior acts as a tourist information centre (open at Easter and April to September). Further along the stroll is the RSPB reserve at North Warren. Take a pair of binoculars – you may see rare birds feeding on the marshes, especially during the migration season. Be prepared to face the bracing North Sea air as you head back along the shingle beach.

The Dolphin

Set in the heart of the small village of Thorpeness, this attractive pub was reopened three years after the original Dolphin Inn had been burnt to the ground in 1994. The new Dolphin has two traditional bars and a smartly refurbished dining room giving a light and bright atmosphere. Outside there is a barbecue area which provides the opportunity for relaxed al fresco dining in the attractive garden during the summer months. Chalked up on a blackboard are details of an ever changing menu with choices such as fisherman's pie, rack of lamb, sage and onion steak, lasagne, gammon, pineapple and chips, scampi and Cumberland sausage with onion gravy. Spotted dick, apple pie and chocolate orange sponge feature among the desserts. Meals may be taken either in the bar areas or in the no-smoking dining room. Drinks include a selection of Adnams real ales and an excellent wine list. If you wish to stay and explore the area, the Dolphin can provide en-suite accommodation. It's best to contact the pub in advance of your visit for details of the opening times, which vary with the seasons. Telephone: 01728 454994.

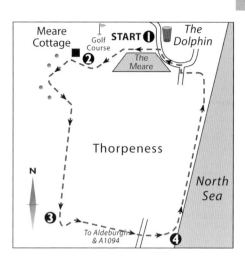

The Walk

① Turn left out of the pub and onto a footway to continue along The Winlands. In about 100 yards turn right to join Upland Road. Carry on along the unmade road, passing the House In The Clouds and the windmill. Continue for about 20 yards on a surfaced stretch and, where the latter bends left, go straight ahead on a narrow path between hedges as waymarked. Skirt the perimeter of a golf course on the right and stay on the path to finally reach Meare Cottage, dated 1882.

The House in the Clouds, Thorpness

The Meare, Thorpness

② Swing left in front of it to join a dismantled railway line (permissive path). On the left are grazing marshes and reedbeds where you might spot migrant wading birds. Keep following the path that runs straight ahead.

③ Pass beside a large metal gate and immediately turn left through a short stretch of bracken. Go over a stile where the sandy path now passes between grassland on either side. When you eventually reach the road ahead, cross straight over and turn left onto stony heathland to walk parallel with the shingle beach.

④ Continue along the Suffolk Coast and Heaths path, keeping to the right of the houses in front. In about another 300 yards past the first house turn left to join a wooden walkway. Go through a car park and turn right onto the road. Just before reaching the village sign, turn left onto a gravel path and walk towards the Meare. Swing right to skirt the latter for a short distance before crossing the road and taking the footway back to the Dolphin.

PLACES OF INTEREST NEARBY

Set in the Elizabethan splendour of **Aldeburgh's Moot Hall Museum**, next to the shoreline, is a collection of the town's ancient artefacts. Displays include Roman cooking pots, a mammoth tusk and an impressive selection of archive photographs. The Moot Hall itself is of historical interest and attracts visitors from far and wide. Telephone: 01728 452158.